THE PRESIDENT AND I

RICHARD NIXON'S RABBI
REVEALS HIS ROLE IN THE SAGA
THAT TRAUMATIZED THE NATION

Rabbi Baruch Korff.

THE PRESIDENT AND I

RICHARD NIXON'S RABBI REVEALS HIS ROLE IN THE SAGA THAT TRAUMATIZED THE NATION

Baruch Korff

Based on the

Rabbi Baruch Korff Archives
John Hay Library, Brown University
Providence, Rhode Island

The Baruch Korff Foundation

Dedication

Parents	Rav Ya'akov Yisroel Korff
	The Zvhiller Rebbe *ZT'L*
	Rabbanit Gittelle Goldman Korff *ZT'L*
	Rabbanit Etta Goldman Korff *ZT'L*
Brother	Rav Shmuel Yitzhak Korff *ZT'L*
Sister and	Adele Korff Gass
Brother-in-law	Max Harry Gass
Sister	Pauline Korff Kerber
Brother-in-law	David Walter Berkowitz
Nephew	David Korff
Niece	Janet Elizabeth Gass
Nephew	Jay Marshall Gass

And extended family of one hundred seventeen souls who died in the Holocaust 1940–45

At my gloomiest, their night-bound voyage was my rudder and sail!

Contents

Preface

For close to two decades, I thought of writing about my relationship with Richard Nixon but couldn't bring myself to relive all the contention. Then, in January 1992, my daughter Zamira, who was then working for the Democratic majority of the Senate Foreign Relations Committee, asked me, "Abba, what did you do wrong?"

Her question, provoked by her associates, persuaded me to face up to the task. I had allowed others to define my role for too long—twenty-nine books from *The Final Days* by Woodward and Bernstein *To Exile* by Robert Sam Anson in my latest count.

Her question was not unlike the four questions she asked each year at the Passover seder, I told Zamira, and the answers provided by the Haggadah, which addresses injustice, are inherent in the answer I have here chronicled to her fifth question.

My initial draft met with mixed reactions. mostly negative. The second and final version, one-third the size of the original, was viewed favorably by some publishers and as unmanageable by others. In two instances I refused to accommodate the bias of editors.

After a year of frustration, I turned to Bob Woodward, who together with Carl Bernstein had authored *The Final Days*. I telephoned him at the *Washington Post* on January 25, 1994. He returned my call the next day and we arranged to meet for lunch on Tuesday February 1, at the Army and Navy Club, where I maintain lodging when in the capital.

I Briefed him between nostalgic reminiscences. He leafed through the manuscript and, like other readers, focused on a reference to the missing 18 1/2 minutes in the crucial Nixon tapes. "Why didn't you . . . Why didn't you follow up on your conversation with Rose Mary Woods?" he asked. I replied, "You are not suggesting that I . . . " "Oh no, no. . . !" he quickly retreated. In light of his expertise on the subject, I suggested that he write a foreword to enhance the book's circulation. He said he would have to consult his wife. He recommended his own agent, Bob Barnett of the Washington law firm Williams and Connolly, to find a suitable publisher for *The President and I*.

An exchange of telephone calls followed between Woodward and me, and Barnett and me. Woodward promised to turn the manuscript over to Barnett. After ten days passed, Barnett called to say he had not received the manuscript from Woodward and would I send another copy to him directly. I didn't. Instead, I called Woodward to trace the whereabouts of the manuscript. He said he was too busy with his current project (The Agenda) to be a "delivery man." The conversation ended on a sour note.

Should the reader find certain parts of my account incompatible with my long-standing affection and regard for Richard Nixon, it is simply because life is not symmetrical. Its rhapsody is not always in tune with events that overtake us.

This is my version of the truth. It is not infallible, but I have tried not to compromise with fact.

Baruch Korff
Providence, Rhode Island
December 1994

PART I
Service to the Presidency

1 Why Fairness

On March 14, 1974, Richard Nixon introduced me to Mayor Richard Daley in the lobby of Chicago's Conrad Hilton Hotel. With outstretched hand, he shouted amid several hundred loyalists, "Meet my rabbi!" A battery of newspeople seized on it, and I've been "Nixon's rabbi" ever since.

How did a retired Orthodox rabbi from New England come to earn that title and the vilification it brought? The story is full of improbabilities, and even today I sometimes have trouble believing it.

It started with the Senate Watergate hearings in 1973. As I watched on television in Rehoboth, Massachusetts, my disbelief grew into disgust, then anger. For four and a half months Nixon's reputation was publicly attacked, and the authority of his presidency weakened, in proceedings that were ostensibly a quest for truth but struck me as nothing more than a clash of political ideologies, an attempt to reverse the 1972 election results. It was a highly one-sided clash as well.

In normal times I would have had little use for the views of much of the coalition arrayed against Nixon during Watergate. I have always leaned to the right politically, though I supported the Democratic candidate in four of the thirteen presidential elections I have voted in. In 1960 and 1968, in fact, I voted for Nixon's opponent.

But the catalyst for me, having spent more than half my life working to rescue Jews around the world, was that Richard Nixon was the single most powerful ally of that cause. In 1972 alone, at his intervention, Leonid Brezhnev released more than 30,000 Soviet Jews, a sixfold increase over the previous rate of exodus. The rate in 1973 was even greater.

Nixon was also the leader of Israel's foremost ally. Preserving the influence of his office was important, then and for the future, not least because of the politics of oil in the Middle East.

There is a classic Jewish concept, derived from the Psalms of David, known as *Hakoras Hatov* (pronounced Ha-KOH-ras Ha-TOVE), or sense of gratitude. The greater the need for help, the greater the obligation to show gratitude for that help. To some Jews, notably the Orthodox, the concept can be a command. Which made more troubling to me the fact that so many Jews were in the anti-Nixon camp.

There have always been differences of opinion among Jews, exacerbated, no doubt, by the lesser-of-grim-evils choices we often face. It's also no secret that we Jews have a tendency to see as black-and-white issues what others might see as shades of gray. We are prophets, not philosophers, for the most part. Accordingly, our disagreements are usually vigorously expressed.

But rescuing Jews is a black-and-white issue to me. So I particularly resented the ingratitude of anti-Nixon Jews. I have always been uncomfortable with the comfortable among my people.

I was also concerned that the powerful forces of antisemitism latent in the United States, most of whose practitioners sided with Nixon politically, could be aroused by the presence of so many Jews in the liberal coalition against him. A rabbi visible in his defense might help defuse those forces and prevent as well a backlash against our alliance with Israel.

Did I think Nixon was innocent of the charges against him? Initially, yes. I saw them as of a piece with the billingsgate that hounded Jefferson and Lincoln and almost drove Washington from office. As an old Massachusetts adage puts it: "Politics ain't beanbag." I ached for what Nixon and his family were going through.

But Watergate was also a textbook study of the choice between means and ends—a choice that has historically divided Jews among themselves and from gentiles. In a very real sense, scrupulousness about means is a luxury. If your family is starving, few would criticize you for stealing food.

Because Jews have been without a safety margin for much of their history, some Jews habitually focus on ends and are tolerant about means. Indeed, Rav Joseph B. Soloveitchik of Boston, the foremost Orthodox talmudic authority of our time, quoted the Babylonian Talmud as follows in defending Nixon: "We do not appoint a communal leader unless he has a can of vermin at his heels [a skeleton in his closet], so that if he should become haughty, we can tell him to turn around [and face his shortcomings]."

Scrupulousness about means is not only justified, it is required when there is a safety margin. That is what being civilized means. But I saw no safety margin during Watergate for the issues that mattered to me. Whether Nixon was guilty or not, therefore, was of limited importance to me. Not only did I tend to believe him, I thought ends took precedence.

So after the *New York Times* rejected a letter I wrote on July 1 defending Nixon, I picked up the phone and persuaded seventeen friends and acquaintances to join me in trying to turn public opinion around. With $1,000 from me, $2,000 from the friends, and a bank loan, in we plunged. The first ad of the National Citizens Committee for Fairness to the Presidency appeared in the *Times* on Sunday July 29, 1973.

2 First Steps

Two days before our first ad ran, John Crewdson of the *New York Times* called to ask whether the White House had anything to do with it. He suspected that presidential aide Charles Colson, another New Englander, was behind it because Colson had had ads placed before, he said, including one entitled "Tell It to Hanoi."

I did my best to disabuse Crewdson of that notion. I cited in particular a disappointing response I had received from presidential counsel Leonard Garment. I had sent Garment a copy of my rejected letter and he replied, "You smote the *Times* smartly. Thanks." But when I wrote him about my idea for a public ad campaign and asked for advice, his response had been, "You should proceed with any plans you have entirely on the basis of your own feelings in the matter."

The first ad was a hasty effort written by Michael S. Kogan of Little Falls, New Jersey, the editor of *Ideas*, a magazine of the John Birch persuasion. But the response exceeded our expectations. In the three days after the ad ran, we received hundreds of calls and approximately 3,000 letters, overwhelming the Rehoboth post office. Half the letters were anti-Nixon, but in the other half were checks and cash totaling close to $30,000. The ad had cost $5,732.

There was evidently a constituency out there waiting to be tapped. We opened Fairness offices in Providence and Washington, D.C. Three weeks after the first ad, our letters were running 90 percent pro-Nixon.

Not all of the unfavorable reactions were political. The reporters and TV crews that descended on Taunton, Massachusetts, to find out about me disturbed the local citizenry, including some members of my old congregation, Agudath Achim, a regional synagogue serving twelve communities.

The *Taunton Daily Gazette* came to our defense in an August 1 editorial by Ted Gay: "Possibly the criticism this group is being subjected to now is another example of why it is difficult for President Nixon to obtain fair treatment from the public."

Another favorable editorial, in the *Boston Herald* on August 2, referred to my "work in rescuing fellow Jews from Nazi Germany." It was sent to Colson, who called to tell me that the President had read it and had said, "Please tell the rabbi that I'm comforted by his experience as a rescuer."

Nixon also asked his secretary, Rose Mary Woods, to sound out Jack Brennan, his military aide, about me. Brennan, a fellow Bay Stater, received a favorable report from the only person on the Fairness Committee he knew, Joseph E. Fernandes of Norton, Massachusetts. Joe was a supermarket chain owner and a prominent local Republican who became the treasurer of Fairness. We had been friends for twenty years.

Later, Rose Mary assuaged my dismay at the inquiry by explaining, "You appeared out of nowhere and everything happened so fast." Also begun was an FBI inquiry into my background, including a review of the information the government already had on me. The inquiry came to light when I passed on to the bureau mail I received threatening the President's life.

The White House staff, I discovered, didn't know what to make of me and decided to try to protect me from pitfalls and the President from my inexperience. Among my chaperones at various times were Patrick Buchanan, Stephen Bull, Charles Colson, Ron Ziegler, Ken Clawson, Bill Baroody, and Bruce Herschensohn, who was installed as liaison with Fairness.

All along I was of the impression that they were just courting me, an impression reinforced by a letter from the President on September 5, 1973. It said in part: "I wanted to thank you personally for stepping forward. . . . Your support at this time reaffirms my belief that . . . the people . . . will help this Administration to achieve the great goals we seek for America and for the world."

My naiveté extended to the impeachment lobby. We were no match for it. The components of that alliance were as different from each other as they were from Richard Nixon. Their ranks included Republicans and Democrats, liberals and conservatives opposed to centrist policies, blue-collar workers and upper-crust activists like Common Cause.

The archdeacon of impeachment, George Meany of the AFL-CIO, had backed Nixon in 1972 but turned against him. Thirteen million copies of the AFL-CIO newspaper were sent out each week giving Meany's views. We repeatedly asked him to allow a one-page ad presenting our side. "No," the archdeacon growled to me, "I want the bastard impeached."

Five million leaflets giving the AFL-CIO's "19 Points for Impeachment" were distributed nationwide, then duplicated in 200 labor magazines and newspapers that reached 12 million homes, according to the union's PR office. All but two of the twenty-one Democrats on the House Judiciary Committee, the body weighing the question of impeachment, received a total of $189,000 from the AFL-CIO for their 1974 reelection campaigns. Another $600,000 went to local unions for campaign activities.

The ACLU and Ralph Nader's Congress Watch enticed the undecided with a million leaflets stressing that impeachment was not conviction, which can only occur after a Senate trial: "Just get the process started." Five organizations manned WATS lines and generated mail chains nationally, the *Washington Star-News* reported.

College students were encouraged to form their own impeachment groups on campus. "Jail to the Chief" pierced the air as the scaffold rose and the noose was braided.

The impeachment lobby spent an estimated $100 million, the AFL-CIO claimed, using an infrastructure that was already in place and largely tax-exempt. Starting from scratch, Fairness raised and spent $3.5 million from its Washington and Providence offices. Local branches expended another $2 million during its one-year existence. The average contribution was $10 at the two main offices and probably about the same at the branches.

Fairness had one paid executive, Barry Cooperstein of Taunton, straight out of college. There were several per diem associates. But all the rest were volunteers. At our busiest, the combination of part-timers and full-timers we had probably amounted to ten full-time workers.

We produced fifteen master ad texts, rotating them from paper to paper. I wrote all but the first, with research help. Our ads appeared in roughly 500 newspapers overall and in virtually every state, including Alaska and Hawaii.

We made our contributor list available to anyone, so some supporters preferred to pay an agency to place an ad, rather than send us a contribution. The agency would call us, and we'd send them a mat that was ready to run.

Once we achieved a national structure of chapters, we sent petitions to our membership for collecting millions of signatures. Copies of the signed petitions went to the White House and to the congressmen in whose districts they were circulated.

We also had chapters file more than 300 complaints with the Federal Communications Commission alleging violations of the Fairness Doctrine by local radio and television stations in their Watergate coverage. As a carrot to go with that stick, we offered the stations messages recorded by the wives of Cabinet officers.

Every now and then, checks would come in from public figures who had not been personally solicited, such as movie actress Anne Baxter and orchestra conductors Leopold Stokowski and Zubin Mehta. When we included Mehta's name in our ads and on our letterhead, however, his business handlers threatened to sue us. We stopped using his name.

3   On the Road

In the beginning several Jews tried to dissuade me directly. When that failed, they told the White House that I was "unrepresentative" and "harmful" to the President's chances for survival. Some members of my family were noticeably cool to me.

Pressure was brought on the rest of the Fairness Committee as well, but we lost only two members—Monsignor Henri Hamel of New Bedford, Massachusetts, and the Rev. Harold Udell, Congregational chaplain at Taunton State Hospital. The remaining sixteen co-founders weathered the fallout and saw our humble beginnings develop into something of a national movement, with more than two million voters enrolled.

The demands of Fairness were such that I eventually had to resign my chaplaincy with the Massachusetts Department of Mental Health and reduce my international activities. Let me explain about those activities.

I began writing speeches for Representative John W. McCormack of Massachusetts, a Democrat, in the late 1930s. Over the years that sideline grew to speechwriting for more than two dozen members of Congress and administration officials, primarily on foreign affairs.

In the 1950s I suggested a U.S. program of scholarships for African students to attend universities in the Middle East to counter the efforts in Africa and the Mideast of graduates of Moscow's Patrice Lumumba University. I soon found myself visiting various heads of state to set up the program, and in my reports afterward, I included profiles of each leader, his aides, and other officials I had met. The profiles were well received and eventually became the primary purpose of further globe-trotting assignments, travels that continue to this day.

I have steadfastly refused to become a government employee, preferring my independence, but one of my passports does say that I travel in the service of the U.S. government. I receive a modest consultant's stipend each time, and part of my expenses is covered by counterpart U.S. funds abroad that can be used only in the country of origin. The access I have achieved leads occasionally to assignments from other countries as well.

As Fairness blanketed the nation with newspaper ads, in the last five months of 1973 alone I made nearly 500 appearances in defense of the President on radio and television and at public gatherings—on occasion as many as five appearances a day.

After I addressed a group on New York's Long Island, a man approached, displayed a concentration camp number on his forearm, and announced to all that I had saved his life. It turns out that he had escaped by means of one of the Paraguayan passports I had pressured the State Department to allow in 1944. His name was Applebaum, one of the random names I had used on the passport forms. He said he had never known how to find me to thank me. It was an emotional encounter, I'll tell you.

There were light moments as well. At a dinner in a school auditorium in Cincinnati, the entrée was ham à la something and the Catholic priest sitting next to me kept urging me to try it: "It's delicious. I won't tell anyone." When my turn came to speak, I told the audience of the priest's advice and promised him, "At your wedding I will taste ham."

Our jousting recalled the time Monsignor Francis McKeon, who was near-sighted, tail-ended my car in Taunton and a policeman asked, "Monsignor, how fast was the rabbi going when he backed into you?" Weeks later I was in the hospital with heart trouble and heavily medicated when I felt Monsignor McKeon's thumb making a cross on my forehead. "Francis," I croaked, "you don't want another collision, do you?"

On my subsequent trips to Cincinnati, Connee Okum, the delightful Catholic housewife who had set up the first gathering, made a point of having kosher food available. She enjoyed kidding her second husband about it: "My first husband, the gentile, knew what the rabbi couldn't eat. This husband, the Jew, doesn't know." Connee earned her Fairness spurs by shaming a department store owner into removing a poster that depicted Nixon in a scatological manner.

Throughout my travels, my hosts by and large were attentive to my dietary needs—particularly the Maynard Schumachers of Humphrey, Nebraska, a German family that was scrupulous on the matter. In 1976 I participated in the Catholic wedding of the Schumachers' son, Paul, in Florida, giving the marital duties from Genesis and a blessing in Hebrew.

On NBC's "Today Show" with Frank McGee, I quoted a talmudic commentary on Ecclesiastes 7:20: "For there is not a righteous man upon earth, that doeth good, and sinneth not." That same day, I received a telegram from Pat Nixon and Julie Eisenhower: "You were tremendous and have our great admiration." It was probably the first time they'd ever applauded anyone who ascribed sin to Richard Nixon.

Later that day, McGee phoned to apologize for having been "out of line." I didn't think he had been. The exchange in question had been one of soul-searching. But his concern touched me deeply. He died of cancer less than three months later. If only I had known! In retrospect I think he was searching for solace.

Another television host whose compassion I appreciated was Dick Cavett. I appeared on his syndicated show with Gore Vidal, who zeroed in on Nixon with withering fire, to audience acclaim. I was immobilized by Vidal's epicene arrogance and wished Bill Buckley were there to help. During intermission Cavett took time to reassure me. "Don't falter," he said. "You have a lot going for you."

The response to my appearances, and the reasons for it, often surprised me. One time Tom Snyder asked me on TV what motivated me. After invoking the Talmud at some length, punctuated by Tom's repeated "How-so's," I finally said, "Tom, haven't you studied the Talmud?" At that point, I later learned, Henry Salvatori, an Italian Catholic from Los Angeles, called the station and left his number for me. He became one of the foremost pillars of Fairness in California.

Jean and Phil Baldwin of El Segundo, California, not only enlisted in the cause, they took my daughter Zamira to Disneyland and all the movie studios. And when threats to my welfare arose, Phil, who is large and imposing, made sure I was never out of his sight during my appearances in the Los Angeles area.

A West Coast corporate executive who prefers anonymity sought me out to say, "Rabbi, I'm a Reform Jew and I don't care for Nixon. But if you want to settle in California and can't find a temple, I'll build you one."

4   The GOP Response

Obtaining support from Republicans was a some-time thing. As chairman of the Republican National Committee, George Bush couldn't commit the party financially. But he quietly encouraged some affluent people to chip in. And he did give Fairness a ringing endorsement in a November 1, 1973, letter to be used for public solicitation.

Ronald Reagan called to say, "I'm in your corner." I thanked him and suggested he enlarge the corner. Sure enough, he sent a sizable contribution and also spoke out for Nixon.

But John Chafee, former Secretary of the Navy under Nixon and a U.S. Senate candidate in Rhode Island in 1972, preferred to distance himself from the White House. I called on Chafee ten days before our first ad ran to ask him to be chairman of Fairness.

"It's too early for any such thing," he said. "I'm afraid to pick up the paper for fear of what I might read. It's ruining the Republican Party."

When I persisted, he said, "I can't be associated with this. It's a dirty business and you shouldn't get involved. Let's wait and see what else comes out."

I said that now was the time to stem the media's anti-Nixon tide.

"They have a lot going for them," he said.

Chafee knew his constituents. At a high school forum in Providence six months later, Cranston Mayor James L. Taft Jr., who had headed Nixon's 1972 reelection campaign in Rhode Island, urged the audience to write to Congress to rid the nation of him. "President Nixon should resign, and if he doesn't, he should be impeached," Taft said.

The other two forum panelists were U.S. Representative Robert O. Tiernan, a Democrat who agreed with Taft, and Providence Councilman Thomas W. Pearlman, a Republican and co-chairman of Fairness, who decried the "mass hysteria" and praised Nixon as "one of the greatest presidents."

Later, in a letter to the House Judiciary Committee, the Providence Monthly Meeting of Friends called for the President's impeachment for "both moral and legal reasons." It didn't help that Nixon himself was a Quaker.

One of our strategies at Fairness was to try to prolong the impeachment process enough to bring the end of Nixon's second term in sight. Perhaps then his foes would back off.

To that end, in September 1973 we filed a class-action suit to have the Senate Watergate hearings shut down. The hearings, we argued, constituted a trial without indictment or jury, usurped the House's power of impeachment, and were destroying the Senate's impartiality as a jury for the President should the House impeach him.

Three months before, Watergate Special Prosecutor Archibald Cox had lost in the same court on one of the specific issues we raised—halting live media coverage of the hearings. Cox, of course, feared damage to a prosecution case against the White House. We sought to protect the White House.

Cox's suit prompted Senator Herman Talmadge of Georgia, a member of the Watergate Committee, to say: "To try to get the judicial branch of the government to enjoin the legislative from functioning is without precedent in the history of the Republic."

In dismissing our suit a week after we filed it, Federal District Judge June J. Green agreed with Talmadge. She even denied Fairness the standing to bring the suit.

5 Official Recognition

On December 19, 1973, the officers of Fairness were invited to the White House before the lighting of the first Chanukah candle. It was my second meeting with Nixon. The first had been in 1967, at his law office, a visit arranged by New England conservatives who wanted me to support him in 1968. He had also phoned and sent a telegram when I retired for health reasons in 1971, and we had exchanged notes in 1972 on the exodus of Soviet Jews.

The President thanked the officers individually as we lined up for picture-taking, and the press and photographers were led in. He then steered me to a desk for a private exchange. "I'm impressed with your messages in the media," he said. "How did you get started?"

I produced a July 30 clipping by David Rogers of the *Boston Globe* that I felt was accurate. Nixon skimmed it and said, "We're being accused of being behind your campaign, which should explain why we kept our official distance. But as of now, you'll get all the cooperation you need." I also showed him our seventh full-page ad, which had just been published.

Then he said, "As you're probably aware, the Vatican wants to see Jerusalem internationalized under the control of the religions that venerate its holy places, something I discouraged. As we speak, Emperor Haile Selassie is leading a delegation to meet the Pope. What do you think? I don't want the issue raised unless it involves a comprehensive peace agreement."

He'd been well briefed on my concerns. Before Israel captured the old part of Jerusalem in 1967 from Jordan, Jews were barred from worshipping at the site of the Holy Temple. I had been more fortunate. On half a dozen occasions between 1960 and 1967, I had worshipped there wearing tallit and tefillin, escorted by Bedouin guards on King Hussein's orders.

After our meeting with the President, I refused to meet with the press lest my comments appear orchestrated by the White House. But I did pass on to Saul Kohler of Newhouse News Service some of Nixon's comments, such as his belief that he was suffering more abuse than his predecessors because news now traveled faster than it used to. And that his daughter Julie called me her rabbi. Kohler reported another comment I provided as follows:

"I'm not a very good Quaker, but my mother was," Nixon said. "I get my inner strength from my mother's faith. We call that the inner peace—peace of mind as well as peace of soul—and this is what gives me my strength."

Several of the Fairness officers lingered for a word with the President. They included attorney Thomas W. Pearlman and insurance executive P. Hoyt Fitch of Providence, Army Major General James C. Fry of Alexandria, Virginia, resort owner Jack Kahn of Sarasota, Florida., jewelry manufacturer Olof V. Anderson of North Kingston, Rhode Island, attorney Edward Cooperstein of Taunton, Massachusetts, and psychotherapist Ernest van den Haag of New York City.

As it turned out, Fairness was one of some fifteen grass-roots pro-Nixon groups that were invited to the White House over several months.

On eight or ten occasions in the ten weeks following our visit, when I was in town, I found myself summoned to the White House for impromptu discussions with the President. An aide would phone: "May we call for you now?" One Friday I chose to walk because it was after sundown, and the President asked why I didn't move to the Hay-Adams Hotel, right across from the White House.

The President's staff began lending a hand in booking my media appearances, although they really didn't have to. Virtually all of my appearances were at the request of recipient groups and media organizations.

At the urging of the White House, I also enlisted Cabinet members and other high-profile figures in the service of Fairness, such as Agriculture Secretary Earl Butz, energy czar and later Treasury Secretary William Simon, Walter Annenberg, former ambassador to Great Britain, and John Volpe, a former Massachusetts governor who was then ambassador to Italy.

But I was never able to persuade the Rev. Billy Graham to join or speak out for the President. "My obligation is to preach the Gospel and not to take sides," he told me, "but I will come and pray with him."

I once reminded Dr. Graham that he had often said that God looks at the sin, not the sinner. "Why then do you distance yourself from Richard Nixon?" I asked. There was a long silence on the phone.

6 The Kendall Caper

Shortly after Fairness's visit to the White House, I got a call from Donald Kendall, chairman of Pepsico, asking me to come see him. I knew he was a friend of the President, through whose intercession he had obtained an exclusive franchise for Pepsi-Cola in the Soviet Union and the Stolichnaya vodka franchise in the United States.

Kendall sent a limousine to LaGuardia Airport to bring me to his corporate headquarters in Purchase, north of New York City. With him was his associate, Cartha DeLoach, former right-hand man of J. Edgar Hoover.

In some detail, I explained how Fairness worked and the plans we had, naming names. Kendall was hospitable and polite and took extensive notes, although he insisted that I sit in a specific chair and that I return to it after I had moved, suggesting that our conversation was being recorded.

He urged me to assume an honorary position and let his people take over. I said that would be okay if it was what the President wanted. But Nixon didn't want me to step aside. He merely wanted a blue-ribbon business presence active in his defense and had told White House aide Peter Flanigan to have Kendall get involved.

The next thing I knew there was a flurry of newspaper ads for something called Americans for the Presidency. Among its supporters were General Lucius Clay, Mamie Eisenhower, Bob Hope, Alf Landon, David Packard, Norman Vincent Peale, George Romney, Eugene Rostow, and Teamsters President Frank Fitzsimmons.

The officers named were Robert E. Bradford, who had called to notify me of the new group, and H. Lee Choate. Kendall was not featured, perhaps for fear of alienating consumers of his products.

In our ad in the *New York Times* on February 22, 1974, Fairness welcomed Americans for the Presidency into the fray. But despite placing full-page ads in more than 100 newspapers through the Washington PR firm of Wagner and Baroody, the new group never took root. Kendall soon met with Flanigan and Bruce Herschensohn at the White House in an attempt to coordinate efforts with Fairness.

Later, Bruce sniffed at "this man's antics," telling me, "He was demeaning of you—not outright, but by gesture and innuendo. Don't depend on him. I think he's a closet anti-Semite, an elitist." Kendall apparently felt that a great many Americans would be "reluctant to join an organization led by a rabbi," so he would start one to accommodate all persuasions.

Only then did I recall that Kendall was rumored to have urged Nixon to ease up on Brezhnev on human rights and the exodus of Soviet Jews. I later learned that Kendall told a mutual associate, "I want to fight for him [Nixon], but I want him to lose."

Bruce was impressed with Bob Bradford, however, and so was I. Bradford was professional and ethical, and when he asked us for a list of our chapters and their principal contacts, I instructed full cooperation with him, despite the mistrust of our people toward any Kendall connection. The Impeachment Express was still rumbling down the tracks. We needed all the help we could get.

The Fairness ad that welcomed Kendall's group also welcomed the National Committee to Support the President, a group headed by Othal Brand, a wealthy Texas farmer. His group soon merged with ours and he proved to be one of Fairness's strongest assets, eventually replacing me as general chairman because we wanted to broaden our appeal to business. All told, we heard from at least half a dozen grass-roots pro-Nixon groups.

Frank Fitzsimmons from the Kendall group became one of our strongest supporters and biggest donors. His blarney sat well with me. "I know the genuine article when I see it," he told me, "and you're it."

7   Gala #1

Four days before our ad welcoming the new groups ran, on the Monday designated as Washington's Birthday, Fairness threw its first gala, a $100-a-plate luncheon in honor of President and Mrs. Nixon. The ballroom of Washington's Mayflower Hotel sported giant portraits of the first and thirty-seventh Presidents, and many guests were left standing when the 457 seats were filled. Hotel staff squeezed in additional tables.

The Secret Service was run ragged. Each guest's credentials had to be verified, and some were turned away, including Nixon biographer Ralph de Toledano, to the consternation of Fairness personnel. Even Cabinet members, whose seats were reserved, were challenged. Treasury Secretary George Shultz was heard to say with some justification, "Well, what can you expect from a bunch of amateurs?"

Vice-President Ford's security detail expressed unhappiness with the "bedlam," and the Secret Service decided that the President should skip the event. I was told that instead the President would host a buffet at the White House after the luncheon, excluding the press.

Cantor Stanley Lipp of my congregation led us all in singing the National Anthem and "God Bless America." (Nothing is so bracing as patriotism with a dash of evangelism!) Speakers included the Vice President, Secretary of Agriculture Earl Butz, and Senators Strom Thurmond of South Carolina and Carl Curtis of Nebraska.

All but Ford, who was presidential, held forth with fire and brimstone. At one point the Vice President advocated "fairness for all, including Congress and everyone else." The response was dead silence. My heart went out to him. He was only a burglar's blunder away from the presidency and no one in the audience wanted him to succeed.

Afterward, buses arranged for by the White House took the guests there, and Fairness staffers and delegation heads helped the Secret Service screen the arrivals. When the President and First Lady appeared in the East Room, the cheers drowned out "Hail to the Chief." The Nixons looked as if they'd been reprieved.

I presented the President with an illuminated scroll and had him give a scroll of appreciation to Elizabeth Mudge, manager of Fairness's Providence office. He drew more cheers by vowing to "stay on my job—the job I was elected to do."

I joined the Nixons in a receiving line as the President shook hands with each guest. One Fairness delegate asked him, "What happened to the eighteen and one-half minutes?" referring to a gap in a White House tape subpoenaed by the Watergate grand jury.

Nixon flushed, and I moved the delegate along. "How did he get in here?" the President muttered.

But Zamira, age six, refused to shake Nixon's hand. "Because of you I don't get to see Abba [Daddy] any more," she told him.

Her mother intervened. "It's time to light the Sabbath candles," she told Zamira.

"Why don't you light the candles here?" the President said. The situation was thus salvaged.

The guests proceeded to the Blue Room for an elaborate buffet. Senior staff from Alexander Haig down circulated and treated the visitors like foreign dignitaries.

The Nixons stayed on, chatting with me. I stood with my hands on my hips for support. It had been a long day, and my back was killing me. When the guests had gone, I took leave of the Nixons and departed with the assistance of a White House staffer.

8   Fairness in Publishing

After a modest rise in the President's standing in the polls following his State of the Union Address, the White House staff embarked on a collaboration with Fairness. On the heels of Washington's Birthday, White House aide Bill Baroody called to say, "The President wants you to do a paperback."

"A what?"

"You heard me. Bruce will be in touch." Bruce Herschensohn, a deputy special assistant to the President, was the right man to influence me. I was very fond of him.

Bill, Bruce, and I met that same day in the office of presidential counselor Anne Armstrong, and to this day I don't know why. We barely discussed the mechanics of putting a book together on short notice. Sensing my dismay, Anne said calmly, "You have to."

She was more interested in Fairness's ability to generate favorable publicity for the President. "How do you manage to pay for all these many ads?" she asked me. "Texas is flooded with them. My mail lately speaks of nothing else."

At my request, Ralph de Toledano contacted several researchers, and a congressional staffer landed the assignment at a cost to Fairness of $1,200. My disappointment in the results was exceeded only by the loss of valuable time. So I handed Toledano a folder of data I had received from the White House, plus my own notes, and asked him to stitch the material together.

Next, I requested an interview with the President for inclusion in the book. I also solicited Vice President Ford for an interview at the urging of the White House. Bruce supplied the title and a description of the author.

Between speaking engagements and ad designing, I kept writing and revising, consulting with the White House on almost every detail. Presidential aide Steve Bull gave me two days' notice for the Nixon interview. I prepared questions as best I could with the assistance of Franklin R. Gannon, aide to Press Secretary Ron Ziegler. After the interview, Gannon wrote me the following:

> This really is an exceptionally informative interview. If you intend to quote it verbatim, or at length, perhaps you will want to edit some of the President's few non sequiturs, repetitions, and incomplete sentences. I have

also marked with paper clips some sections which, although true, might be questioned for reasons of taste or legality. May I say that you are doing a noble job, against great odds.

We worked it out between us and added a supplement of written questions and answers two weeks later.

But no one would publish it. Two publishers were willing but couldn't meet our deadline. "Even if we could," one said, "it may be too late to be of any commercial value."

The finished product had to be on the stands by the third week in June, to compete with the impeachment surge by the House Judiciary Committee and to meet the schedule of events Fairness had planned. We had no alternative but to publish it ourselves, which we did—300,000 copies—with all the accompanying errors of haste and inexperience.

Fairness Publishers did have a distinctive owl logo, however, drawn by Barbara Russell of Washington, D.C., whose husband, Edward, was the younger brother of Lord Ampthill of England. When I asked why an owl, Barbara replied, "Because, Baruch, it can see in the dark."

Support for President Nixon wasn't the only reason Barbara had joined Fairness. Her maiden name was Korff, a name that had originated, she said, on the island of Corfu, off the coast of Albania and Greece.

Her Korffs had embraced the Russian Orthodox Church in the nineteenth century and her father had been appointed governor-general of Finland by the last czar. He escaped to this country in 1917 during the Russian Revolution and founded the School of International Relations at Georgetown University. Another branch of the Korffs, she said, had joined the Lutheran Church in Germany. A Baron deKorff had been finance minister there under Bismarck.

· · ·

In mid-March, the President went on the road for a week to shore up his support. Fairness tried to make him feel welcome and the media aware of it. In Chicago, Paul Shoemaker and General Julius Klein turned out an enthusiastic crowd in the Hilton lobby and sent a dozen well-dressed supporters with homemade signs outside to counter a couple of anti-Nixon pickets on the sidewalk.

We made similar efforts for the President's visits to the Grand Ole Opry in Nashville and the Space Center in Houston. In Houston he had to deal with questions about the call for his resignation by conservative Senator James Buckley, Bill's brother.

In April the Internal Revenue Service ruled that the President owed $432,787 in back taxes, plus interest. He said he would pay it, and Fairness began to receive contributions earmarked for his taxes. So did the White House and the IRS, as well as conservative Chicago radio personality Paul Harvey and others.

"We have never had a case like this before," an IRS official was quoted as saying. One group reportedly offered to foot the entire bill in return for some of Nixon's vice-presidential and presidential papers, which would be given to a university in the Southwest.

The President ordered all contributions returned with thanks, but not all had return addresses. The White House said it would give its unreturnable gifts to charity. The IRS gave its to the U.S. Treasury's general fund. At Fairness, we returned those we could and sent the others to the White House. I don't recall how much was involved in all. One published report attributed to a White House source a figure of $40,000 for Fairness. That strikes me as too high.

During Passover 1974, Julie Eisenhower took the trouble to arrange a kosher luncheon at the White House with advice from a local rabbi. The guests included Dr. John McLaughlin, a Jesuit priest who was a Nixon speechwriter; presidential assistant Pat Buchanan; Ken Clawson, deputy director of White House communications; Bruce Herschensohn; Rebecca, Zamira, and me.

It was to have been a strategy session but was mostly sound and fury. At one point I found myself staring over the matzo-ball soup at Buchanan's accusatory finger and being told, "You are preaching to the choir."

The event was not without benefit, however. It gave me an insight into Julie that is conveyed by the following impressions Rebecca wrote down later that day:

April 11, 1974, 10 p.m. From the time I left the W.H. at nearly 3 p.m. I've been in a state of suspension, dazed by the dialogue at the luncheon and depressed by Julie's appearance. She seemed emaciated, bewildered, grasping at straws amid adults who confessed to having no strategy and that no thought was given as to the tapes promised to the Judiciary Committee two weeks ago. There was an air of inadequacy [as with people] stranded in a ship [without] rudder, sail, [or] compass.

What was so depressing [were] the accounts of the men, all defensive, on how they withstood the on-slaughts, begging the question. Among the saddest of all remarks [were]:

—"We must have a strategy" (Herschensohn).

—"We promised the Judiciary Committee two weeks ago they would have the tapes in two weeks, but we haven't prepared for an extension of the two weeks" (Buchanan).

—"How do you answer the question about the [Howard] Hughes money going to Rose Mary Woods and to the President's brother?" (Clawson).

—"We really should find out exactly what's on those tapes" (McLaughlin).

A pall hung around them, and when I proposed a posture of attack rather than dealing with detailed charges, I was looked upon with amazement. I felt naive, like a novice among guilt-laden individuals.

Still, I turned from Julie, unable to look at her [without] breaking down in pity and sorrow for what this fragile girl must endure. The feeling that they know more than I do kept mounting within me and a sense of hopelessness gripped me each time I sought to dispel the gloom. I suddenly felt . . . as if I were at a wake before an open bier.

Yet there they were—Pat Buchanan, a gifted ideologue; Ken Clawson, a shrewd strategist of enormous potential; Bruce Herschensohn, who wears his soul on his face, loyal, dedicated, enterprising, and talented; and McLaughlin, whose zeal for politics is outstripped by his church anchorage. All caught in the currents of history not of their making, with not a single life raft aboard the wreckage called "Watergate."

Again, I found myself facing Julie and my heart sank. There I was again a captive of this frail human being reaching out for a life raft and I had none to offer. . . . [In] her eyes I gleaned despair, and yet there was a greater perception in her every nuance than among those who shared her hospitality. Unable to conceal her pain, she nevertheless held out the only hope visible at the table, as if she were the sole custodian of weaponry inaccessible to others.

After that luncheon, Julie became a singular force that propelled me. From the beginning, I had seen her as the President's best weapon—admirable and utterly believable but for her filial tie. Indeed, the fourth full-page ad of the Fairness series, introduced on September 9, 1973, was an open letter to her:

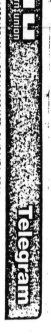

Western Union Telegram

PDA030(0846)(1-003111C024)PD 01/24/74 0846

ICS TPMWAWH WSH

08009 GOVT THEWHITEHOUSE DC 21 01-24 834A EDT

PMS RABBI BARUCH KORFF

NATIONAL CITIZENS COMMITTEE FOR FAIRNESS TO THE PRESIDENT

18 INDUSTRIAL BANK BLDG

PROVIDENCE RI 02907

WE HAVE JUST WATCHED YOUR APPEARANCE ON THE TODAY SHOW. YOU WERE

TREMENDOUS AND HAVE OUR GREAT ADMIRATION

PAT NIXON AND JULIE EISENHOWER

NNNN

AF-1201 (R5-69)

Telegram from Pat Nixon and Julie Eisenhower about Korff's appearance on Today show, Jan. 24, 1974.

9 A Letter to Julie

Dear Julie,

Like many Americans, I am deeply moved by your marathon "defense" of your illustrious father and impressed with your eloquence even in inhospitable environments. Still, it must be a terrible ordeal for you to have to suppress your anger and frustrations at the unfairness of it all. You must have felt more than once like exploding with indignation at the purveyors of political pornography who are gnawing at your father and tearing at the very fabric of our nation.

You must know, however, that character assassination is not new in the annals of the presidency. The "Father of his Country" was similarly reviled. As Rupert Hughes asks, "Of what infamy was Washington not falsely accused during his lifetime?" I am not asking you to take comfort in the travail of your father's predecessors; what I am suggesting is that there are inescapable hazards that come with the office, hazards that have multiplied with time.

In a letter to Thomas Jefferson, George Washington complained that his enemies "have embraced without restraint every opportunity to weaken the confidence of the people" in him. At one time, according to Jerome Davis, author of *Character Assassination*, "criticism was so scathing and so unfair that Washington declared that he would rather be in the grave than in the Presidency."

The Pentagon and SALT thefts and the purloined Grand Jury minutes may have had their genesis in the birth of our nation. The first President discovered that some of his own personal letters were intercepted and read. Having learned of this, he wrote to Hamilton: "About the middle of last week I wrote to you: and that it might escape the eye of the Inquisitive (for some of my letters have been lately pried into) I took the liberty of putting it under cover to Mr. Jay."

Washington often reflected on the "malignant industry, and preserving falsehoods" with which he was assailed. His countrymen, however, eventually bestowed upon him the highest honor within their power: "Father of his Country." And while the office has its perils as well as its rewards, the tragedy is that the perils come to the President when he is alive and the rewards come to him when he is dead.

The *Porcupine* of January 29, 1798, referred to "the mean and cowardly conduct of Mr. Jefferson," while a Massachusetts paper described Jefferson and his supporters as "desperate, embarrassed, unprincipled, disorderly, ambitious, disaffected, morose men."

Jefferson's daughter, Martha, must have buried her head in her pillow while reading of her father's disgust with "the malignant passions of politics and party hatreds that seem like salamanders to consider fire as their element." And yet, my dear Julie, time served to elevate Thomas Jefferson to "one of the loftiest pinnacles in American history," and so time, too, will raise your father in the eyes of his countrymen to great heights, and, by the grace of God, during his lifetime.

To close my letter to you without citing some of the epithets hurled upon Lincoln would be unthinkable. Few Presidents, your father included, have been more maligned than Abraham Lincoln. A journalist, Henry Villard, accused Lincoln of "a fondness for low stories. He seemed bent upon making his hit by fair means or foul. . . . Again and again, I felt disgust and humiliation that such a person should have been called upon to direct the destinies of a great nation." With unrestrained fury, Lincoln's detractors called him "a hater of the Constitution" and accused him of being "pledged to subvert it." Doesn't this have a familiar ring to it? Similarly, the *New York World* charged Lincoln with "polluting the fountains of justice instead of cleaning the Augean stables." Lincoln still lives as one of the greatest Presidents, while his tormentors barely occupy a footnote to history. So it shall be with your father— a man who towered above his detractors and prevailed; and, by the grace of God, during his lifetime.

A cursory look at the unholy alliance arrayed against your father brings to mind one of President Cleveland's slogans, "We love him for the enemies he has made": A. O. Sulzberger, Shannon and Lewis of the *New York Times*, Maddox of Georgia, Rather of CBS, Amin of Uganda, Kiker of NBC, Schmitz of California, and Graham of the *Washington Post* are but a handful of the cadre with a penchant for "Seven Days in May."

Take heart, my dear Julie, and be of good courage; the tide is turning in favor of your father. Your grandchildren will one day look back with pride at a great-grandfather who, like his predecessors, rose above the calumny of his time.

With kindred spirit,
Baruch Korff

An old adage would have us "tell a parent by the child." My appraisal of the President drew from both father and daughter, and my friendship with Julie continued well after her father's pardon. I dined with David Eisenhower and her at their Washington apartment, where I saw the holes and defacements in the walls created when the Secret Service removed the security system they were no longer entitled to.

10 Playing Beanbag

"Every yokel who pipes up with a prediction that Nixon will resign in two or three weeks makes headlines. It's coming—Hallelujah!" wrote Dorsey Short in the *Ridgewood* (N.J.) *Times* on April 25. As the ship of state continued to spring leaks, Fairness tried to plug every one. Here is a note I wrote to Alexander Haig, Nixon's chief of staff, on May 7:

> I was terribly distressed at a front-page story in today's *Post* wherein a member of the White House staff is quoted as saying, "For the first time, I no longer think that the President is going to make it." It would appear that the old Jewish adage "Save me, O God, from my friends and let me worry about my enemies" is applicable. . . . I hope this son of a bitch is ferreted out and thrown out on his ear. Please don't be startled at the language—you'll find it in the Bible. . . . We have enough to overcome without sabotage from within.

I later learned from a *Washington Post* reporter that Haig himself had been the staffer in question. In our impromptu meetings at the White House, the President had alluded to an "in-house coup" feeding on an external plot to unseat him. He suggested the involvement of top intelligence operatives, then said, "Paranoia is not an impeachable offense."

Specifically, Nixon was scornful of the testimony of former CIA Director Richard Helms, considering "the many times we pulled his chestnuts out of the fire." Helms told several Senate panels in 1973 that he had resisted White House efforts to get the CIA to play a role in the Watergate coverup. Indeed, Nixon had fired Helms right after the 1972 election, and Helms felt that his lack of cooperation in the coverup had been the cause, according to his biography.

The President also speculated on Alexander Butterfield's possible associations with the CIA. Butterfield, a retired Air Force officer who was in charge of the White House taping system, had revealed its existence in July 1973, in response to a direct question by the minority counsel for the Senate Watergate Committee Fred Thompson of Tennessee, newly elected to the U.S. Senate with the Republican surge in November 1994 election.

Former White House Counsel John Dean's testimony had earlier raised the possibility of such a system. In addition, at Nixon's behest, special counsel Fred Buzhardt had leaked summaries of the Nixon-Dean conversations to the Senate Watergate Committee's minority staff. The summaries were based on the tapes and had struck the staff as far too detailed for normal recall.

Butterfield's testimony earned him the lasting enmity of Rose Mary Woods, who called him an unprintable name and told him, "You are on the other side."

Impeachment sentiment grew after the President released to the Judiciary Committee heavily edited transcripts of forty-six White House tapes. The 1,300-plus pages made public on April 30, 1974, introduced "expletive deleted" to the language and conveyed an Oval Office image that was anything but statesmanlike. Conservative columnist Joseph Alsop likened it to "the back room of a second-rate advertising agency in a suburb from hell."

It didn't help that nearly two-thirds of the 2,200-odd omissions in the transcripts, made on grounds of unintelligibility or irrelevance, occurred while the President was speaking. Or that the Judiciary Committee's own transcripts of eight tapes in its possession differed occasionally from the White House transcripts of those tapes, with the latter version usually favoring the President.

There were also several large omissions not identified as such in the Administration's transcripts, including a 2,500-word section during which the President had said, "I want you all to stonewall it, let them plead the Fifth Amendment, cover up, or anything else, if it'll save it—save the plan."

The public was hardly indifferent. All 350,000 words

of the White House transcripts were run in full by some fifty newspapers, and two paperbacks of the transcripts were rushed into print and became instant best-sellers—with a combined publication run ten times the size of my paperback.

The lone bright spot for the Administration was the acquittal of former Cabinet members John Mitchell and Maurice Stans by a federal jury in New York City two days before the White House transcripts were released. They had been charged with impeding an investigation by the Securities and Exchange Commission in return for a contribution to Nixon's 1972 campaign. Among the witnesses not believed by the jury was John Dean, the President's chief accuser.

The Nixon-sinking predictions were intended to force him to resign rather than to bring about his impeachment, which would have claimed more casualties in the Senate and House. With this in mind, Fairness petitioned the Justice Department to investigate the impeachment lobby—including the AFL-CIO, Common Cause, the ACLU, and affiliates of consumer advocate Ralph Nader—for abuses of the tax-exempt privilege, which does not encompass partisan politics.

We included the Fairness Committee on the list of targets for cosmetic purposes, since we had no such privilege. Our petition also called for an investigation of the use of the franking privilege by members of Congress opposed to Nixon.

But the petition was doomed from the start. The Justice Department indicated privately that it would be rejected, and it was. I thought this was a serious mistake. For fear of appearing to use public office for partisan purposes, the Administration conceded the game to partisans out of office. Focusing on means forfeited the ends.

The same thing had happened with Vice President Spiro Agnew. The impeachment lobby wanted no part of him succeeding Nixon. So the White House cooperated! At Nixon's urging, Agnew resigned pursuant to a no-contest plea in federal court in October 1973 for tax evasion, part of an investigation into kickbacks he was charged with taking as governor of Maryland.

Had Agnew gone through impeachment himself, action against Nixon might have been delayed long enough to enable him to last out his term. Yes, an indicted Vice President is an embarrassment to country and party. And at the time Nixon probably thought that cutting Agnew loose as quickly as possible was necessary to holding his Republican base in Congress.

But it didn't work out that way; and that particular exercise in means priority, I thought, significantly abetted the worse result that did occur—a weakened presidency because Richard Nixon had to resign. Politics ain't beanbag.

11   Gala #2

Fairness soldiered on. On June 9, we assembled some 1,800 delegates from forty-five states for a luncheon at Washington's Shoreham Hotel to honor the Nixon family. The crowd exceeded the official capacity of the hotel's Regency Ballroom by at least 200. The gathering enabled delegates to lobby their representatives as well.

As the head table guests lined up to march in to the music of Lionel Hampton, President and Mrs. Nixon and I were held back for a climactic entrance. I was chatting with Mrs. Nixon when the President tugged at my sleeve and said rather shyly, "There's not much time left. Call out your troops. Let the Supreme Court know that many Americans back their President." Because of the hoopla, his message did not sink in until later. "Let the Supreme Court know . . ." In six weeks the court would rule on the President's claim of absolute privilege to withhold evidence subpoenaed by the Watergate prosecutor.

As the First Couple entered, the orchestra struck up "Hail to the Chief," and the applause was thunderous. Some guests danced in the aisles. Syndicated columnist Nick Thimmesch captured the flavor of the assembly this way:

> They were the Faithful, radiating righteousness, feeling a bit persecuted as Mr. Nixon's defenders, led by a battle-worn rabbi, not by the slick machine which reelected the President...
>
> The speakers seemed to find it necessary to cry out their religious affiliation, in contrast, perhaps, to the Orthodox Judaism of Rabbi Korff, who has to be admired for his demand for justice.
>
> [Quoting Othal Brand,] "A movement which has a Texas Baptist farmer like me as general chairman . . . and an old-fashioned rabbi as president has gotta be grass-roots." A moment later Rabbi Korff told the faithful, "I feel fulfillment because between us (he and Brand) we have heaven and earth."
>
> [Father Franz-Bernard Lickteig, a Carmelite from Washington, D.C.] eulogized Mrs. Patricia Nixon for her strength in adversity. Father Lickteig's remarks brought enormous applause, which he tried to stop with "This is not a speech, but a sermon."...
>
> On and on it went, the people earnest and impassioned. It all could have fit into a revival tent. When it was over, I didn't feel the need to go to church that Sunday.

Other speakers included Sen. Carl Curtis of Nebraska, Ambassador John Volpe, and Tricia Nixon Cox. The President's speech at the luncheon focused on foreign policy and was stirring. He spoke of the trip he and Mrs. Nixon would embark on the next day to the Mideast—15,000 miles" to "five nations"—"difficult trip from the physical standpoint" and for "the diplomacy involved."

He said he had visited more than "80 countries over the past 27 years" and that "each of these journeys contributes to a goal which is far in the future and one which we must constantly work to achieve." The United States, he said, seeks to assure "every nation on the globe the right to independence, the right to security, the right to seek their own way to achieve their own goals. This is the American foreign policy in a nutshell."

"In the past five years," he said, "we have seen the whole world change for the better: the end of a long war and ending it with the respect and honor . . . essential for a great power if it is to be a leader after; the opening of communication with China; the opening of negotiations with the Soviet Union. . . . Whoever is the American President will hold in his hands the responsibility for building on the great initiatives that we have begun."

He praised Fairness for standing up for "the office of the presidency"—"what is involved in the future is the American presidency and what it can do not only for Americans but for all the people who inhabit this globe... [A] strong American presidency is essential if we are to have peace in the world."

He closed by quoting from a letter he said hung on the office wall of a stenographer in the Executive Office Building, written by her boss: "We have been together ever since we came to Washington in 1969 as part of this great adventure, on Jan. 20 of that year, and we shall leave together only when we have completed our service—heads high on Jan. 20, 1977... There remains much to be done—believe me, with your help we are going to do the job."

In retrospect, the speech gave me much to ponder. On the physical difficulty of the trip, his physician, Dr. Walter Tkach, later told me: "He took a calculated risk. It could have killed him." Did he wish that? Or did the trip itself and what "remains to be done" indicate a yearning to prolong his lease on the White House and wistfulness about its impending loss? And why attribute to a stenographer's boss a vow—to leave only when his term was up—that he had expressed directly many times before? Was "believe me" the kind of intensifier we all invoke when we know the point we want accepted is tenuous?

In two months to the day, he would vacate the White House. Did he know then? "There's not much time left," he'd said to me. "Call out your troops."

12 In Convention Assembled

So call out the troops I did, sounding an SOS to all of our 231 chapters and support groups to come show the flag in the nation's capital.

The need for speed galvanized everyone. Our headquarters overseer, Barry Cooperstein, worked the phones day and night. Paul Shoemaker of Chicago and Grace Montgomery of Alexandria, Virginia, supervisor of office volunteers, focused on communication networks. Paul Schumacher and his parents, Maynard and Rita, and Connee Okum, together with W. Clement Stone of Chicago, arranged transportation with Stone's generosity. Barbara and Edward Russell and Admiral Elliott B. Strauss mailed the faithful lobbying material to be sent to the Hill.

*Friday, February 22, 1974, Korff with the Nixons in thought and
conversation following a reception at the White House.*

Rabbi Korff
Sorts It Out

By Haynes Johnson
Washington Post Staff Writer

It's the ingratitude, he says, over and over, the ingratitude and the inequity that are "literally driving me out of my mind." And don't misunderstand, he says, again and again, when he speaks of no longer being able to go home, of the insults and humiliations and severed friendships, he's not seeking sympathy.

"I want to again caution you," he says, in those measured tones, with that heavy accent. "I don't want any sympathy. I don't want any headlines. There will always be those who will say, 'Well, he's naive, he's a fool, he shouldn't have gotten into it.' I do not regret, not the slightest, what I have done. I think that at least everyone is entitled to one defender."

Rabbi Baruch Korff's is one of the last of the Watergate stories. He insists his case differs markedly—he

See **RABBI, A8, Col. 3**

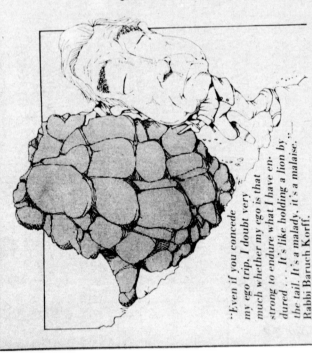

"Even if you concede my ego trip, I doubt very much whether my ego is that strong to endure what I have endured . . . It's like holding a lion by the tail. It's a malady, it's a malaise."
Rabbi Baruch Korff.

By John Twohey—The Washington Post

Cartoon by John Twohey in the Washington Post.

Nixon and Korff at the White House, December 1973.

Nixon and the author in the Oval Office, March 13, 1974. Nixon's two-hour conversation with Korff on this occasion, reprinted in the appendix, was his last interview as President.

Baruch Korff, Richard Nixon, and Nixon son-in-law Ed Cox at dinner honoring Nixon family, Shoreham Hotel, Washington, June 9, 1974.

Korff presenting Nixon with a copy of the paperback edition of The Personal Nixon, *San Clemente, July 16, 1974. Nixon wrote the following inscription: "To Rabbi Korff, for whose friendship, support and wise counsel I shall always be grateful."*

Treasury Secretary William Simon, Mrs. Nixon, and Korff at the Fairness to the Presidency convention, Shoreham Hotel, Washington, July 18, 1974.

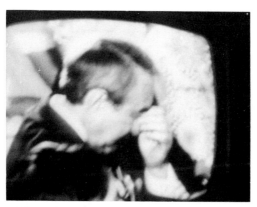

Korff's tearful reaction to Nixon's farewell to the cabinet and White House staff was captured on the TV tube on the morning of August 9, 1974.

Korff and President Anwar Sadat of Egypt at his palace in Alexandria, May 1978.

President Anwar Sadat, left, *and Vice President Hosni Mubarak,* second from right, *blessing Zamira Korff. May 1978.*

Admiral Elliott B. Strauss, a principal figure in the Fairness Campaign.

Senator Orrin G. Hatch with Rabbi Baruch Korff, senior legislative advisor, and Colonel Terry L. Paul, senate liaison officer, in flight over the Balkans on a Marine Corps jet in 1990.

Rabbi Korff, right, reads Scroll of Honor to Senator Carl T. Curtis of Nebraska at Perspectives dinner. Looking on, left to right: Senator Edward Zorinsky, Senator Curtis, Senator Howard H. Baker, Jr., Senator Russell B. Long, Senator James A. McClure, Representative James R. Mann, Senator Clifford P. Hansen.

Right, *Senator Claiborne Pell, outgoing Democratic chairman of Senate Foreign Relations Committee, and, left, Senator Jesse Helms, incoming Republican chairman, with Rabbi Korff at a reception in 1994 at the office of Senator Robert Dole promoting the American-Israeli Promenade to be developed in Telz-Stone, on the outskirts of Jerusalem.*

Baruch Korff, accompanied by General Uzi Narkis, at Yad Vashem Holocaust Memorial, Jerusalem, seeking names of martyred kin. October 1994.

Anwar Sadat with Ellen and Melvin Heller of New York who accompanied the author on one of his visits with the Egyptian President. The Heller's philanthropy extended even to the Nile.

Howard R. Swearer, President of Brown University at the dedication of the Rabbi Baruch Korff Archives, November 4, 1985. In his introduction in the exhibition catalogue Dr. Swearer stated: "We are deeply indebted to Rabbi Baruch Korff for making Brown University the repository of his lifelong collection of papers and memorabilia. This is a major addition to the University's archival library and a treasure trove for the historian and researcher."

**Republican
National
Committee**

George Bush, Chairman

November 1, 1973

Rabbi Baruch Korff
National Citizens Committee
for Fairness to the Presidency
618 Industrial Bank Building
Providence, R. I. 02903

Dear Rabbi Korff and other leaders:

The National Committee strongly supports
your efforts to see that the President of the
United States is accorded fair play. We are
not in a position to send cash. We are in a
position to commend you on what you are doing
to strongly urge that Republicans and Democrats
alike give support to your move to place matters
into their proper perspective, and to demonstrate
to this country - and indeed to the world - that
our President has an enormous resource of support
and goodwill.

Thank you for the telegram you sent me.

Yours very truly,

George Bush

Dwight D. Eisenhower Republican Center: 310 First Street Southeast, Washington, D.C. 20003 (202) 484-6700

Letter from George Bush, chairman of the Republican National Committee, endorsing the National Citizens Committee for Fairness to the Presidency, Nov. 1, 1973.

ראש הממשלה

ירושלים,   ה' בשבט תשל"ח
13 בינואר 1978

8-9184

לכבוד
הרב ברוך קורף
בית מדרש רחובות
<u>רחובות, מסצ'וסטס</u>

הרב קורף הנכבד,

עלי לבקש את סליחתך על האיחור במתן תשובתי למכתבך האחרון.
הוא הונח על שולחני אך הבוקר.   כבודו בודאי יודע את סיבת האיחור,
הקשור במתן מענה למכתבים אישיים.   השבועות האחרונים היו מוקדשים
למאמץ העיקרי של ישראל, המשא ומתן על תנאי השלום וכל מה שכרוך
בו.

דברי הידידות שלך יקרים לי מאד.   הדו"ח על השיחה עם השאח,
מאשר את הרשמים שקיבלנו על עמדתו, במישרין.

בכבוד רב,

מ. בגין

Letter to Korff from Israeli Prime Minister Menachem Begin, Jan. 13,
1978.

Othal Brand, whose election as general chairman of Fairness had freed me to focus on the Judiciary Committee, speaking engagements, and newspaper ads, was in charge of logistics. In the words of Mildred Stein, wife of the President's economic advisor, Brand was "God-sent." As a leading trader in produce—he owned more than 2 million acres of farmland in Mexico—he was skilled in negotiating every impasse. He once shipped two boatloads of onions to Iran with assistance from my contacts.

Nothing discouraged Brand. When Fairness needed a security and surveillance system for its offices, he called an aide in Texas and told him to send Joe Fernandes an amount that covered it. "The hole of a needle can accommodate friends," he declared. Of the White House's occasional despair, he would say, "This is a retreat from God, a haven for self-pity."

Brand commuted between Texas and Washington as if they were across town from each other. A Baptist missionary by avocation, he sponsored his 75-member church choir for the turnout.

And so it went day after day until Thursday, July 18, when Fairness opened a five-day convention with a $10-a-plate dinner at Washington's Shoreham-Americana Hotel. There were near-heartbreaks, such as the contingents from Wichita and Salt Lake City, which were not expected to make it but did.

In all, more than 2,000 people attended, including "the President's favorite choir," a 90-member African-American group from the Cathedral of Faith in Inkster,

Michigan, and their minister, Dr. Herbert Hinkle. At Dr. Hinkle's urging, the gathering shouted, "Love is here!"

The gala was described by one newsman as a "solemn high mass of patriotism." Lionel Hampton's orchestra complemented the vocalizing of both choirs with style and grace. Hampton played a song he had written called "We Need Nixon," and the crowd sang the words:

We need Nixon,
We need Nixon,
Let's stay with Nixon,
Please stay with Nixon,
Let's help him finish the job.
With faith and love we'll place our trust.
People know him,
Our man is Nixon,
So let's all show him
He's right on fixin'
A better world for all of us.
We're sure that he's the best man for the job.

The "congregation"—a diverse blend of the ethnic, racial, religious, and cultural—was a family united in its support for the President. The only skeptics present were at the press tables, and the hostility toward them in the room was palpable. When Anne Armstrong chided the media for insisting that the President reveal his "most secret conversations" while claiming confidentiality for their "reliable sources," the applause was prolonged.

One "middle-aged woman from St. Louis," wrote columnist Mary McGrory, "leaned over to the press table and said grimly, 'You're lucky you're in a civilized country.'" Another woman "glared at a reporter" and said, "You are crucifying him without a cross, do you know that?" Miss McGrory was surprised at the "generous sprinkling of blacks" in the audience, "some of whom brought their small children."

Besides Ms. Armstrong, the speakers included Julie Eisenhower, Secretary Butz, Senator Curtis, and me. The President remained at the Western White House but spoke to the gathering by phone. The crowd chanted, "We Love Nixon." Mrs. Nixon, Tricia and Ed Cox, and David Eisenhower were present. Cabinet members and White House staffers also attended. They were supportive but cheerless.

The convention's five-day agenda included luncheons for each Fairness delegation with its state representatives and lobbying in the halls of Congress. Summations before the House Judiciary Committee had begun Thursday. Debate on impeachment would occur the following week, with voting immediately after.

On Friday some 350 of us, mostly the younger members, went to the Capitol building. A dozen antiwar protesters were on the steps with a life-size model of one of the "tiger cages" that North Vietnam kept prisoners in. After being made to leave our signs outside, we entered the Rotunda. Seven flights of scaffolding lined it, and all its statues were wrapped in plastic.

There we sang "America the Beautiful," "The Battle Hymn of the Republic," and "The Power and the Glory," complete with handclapping, using songbooks we'd distributed. The security guards said they would have to arrest me if we didn't stop, so on the promise that House Speaker Carl Albert would join us outside on the steps, we left after singing "My Country, 'Tis of Thee."

One benefit of moving outside, I felt, was that it would help disassociate Fairness from the Moonies, who had joined our protest. I was told that the Rev. Sun Myung Moon himself had arrived. I was always wary of giving the media any extraneous basis for criticizing our efforts. I later learned that the Moonies had asked to join us and had received permission

Dozens of us then went back inside to lobby anyone we could. I led prayers against impeachment outside the Judiciary Committee room while Committee Counsel John Doar was introducing the articles of impeachment inside. As the members emerged from their deliberations, Haynes Johnson of the *Washington Post* reported,

> they were met by a number of vocal Nixon supporters. . . . In the clamor of that crowd one woman wearing a badge identifying herself as a member of the "Citizens Congress for Fairness to the President" said: "We elected him President, and he has the right to use his judgment on what he should break into."

Our local affiliates used several variations on the fairness theme for their own names. On Saturday evening we marched by candlelight to the Lincoln Memorial, singing patriotic songs and spelling out N-I-X-O-N with our formation on the steps in hopes of attracting media cameras. On Sunday some of us picketed the CBS News Bureau offices for not covering us. On Monday we began a three-day prayer vigil at the Capitol building.

On Wednesday, July 24, the Supreme Court unanimously ruled against the President's claim of absolute privilege regarding the White House tapes. Debate on the impeachment articles began in the Judiciary Committee the same day.

Fairness was not the only participant concerned with timing. On Thursday, July 18, the *Washington Post* ran an unflattering eight-column profile of me by Sally Quinn. My naiveté was only partly to blame.

Miss Quinn's theme was that I must have an angle. My defense of the President couldn't simply be a matter of belief. Nixon himself had doubts about my motives, she wrote, and had assigned Bill Baroody to monitor my actions. She had followed me for several days with pad and pen, and Baroody had sat in on many of our sessions.

Her profile emphasized my considerable ego, which is fair enough, but put words in my mouth that I never use, such as "darling." Worse, in quoting me on my preference for patriarchal, not matriarchal, families, she chose not to report my biblical citations nor the example I gave of the tolerant way the Israeli Knesset handled the polygamy of the Yemenite Jews who came to Israel during Operation Magic Carpet in 1949.

Instead, the blonde Miss Quinn made it appear that I believed in philandering and was trying to chat her up. Neither could be farther from the truth, particularly the second.

Fortunately, the article merely increased Fairness's anger at the press, though a woman from Tennessee did tell me at the banquet, "You're quite a man." Othal Brand and Joe Fernandes expressed sympathy with "the cross I had to bear," as did others who knew me well. When the profile appeared in the *Boston Globe* two weeks later, my brother Samuel was moved to write a letter to the editor.

Miss Quinn's response to my objections was to suggest that I, too, write a letter to the editor. Two years later, however, at a low point for me personally, I happened to be talking with Ben Bradlee, the *Post*'s legendary editor and Miss Quinn's companion, one of several talks I had with Bradlee over the years. Afterward, he sent star reporter Haynes Johnson to interview me. The result was a sympathetic profile that ran on page one.

My paperback, *The Personal Nixon: Staying on the Summit,* made its debut at the gala, a change in timing we decided on after the President urged me to call out the troops. On July 15 I had taken two copies to San Clemente, given one to the President the next day, and faced the press in all its variety.

Picking up on my description of myself as a "small-town rabbi," UPI reporter Helen Thomas asked, "Did you say small rabbi or small-town?" Phil Shabecoff of the *New York Times*, on the other hand, asked a series of intelligent questions, then requested the remaining copy of the paperback. I readily complied. He apparently recognized the value of what might be Nixon's final extensive interview as President.

Shabecoff called later that day to ask what I would charge the *Times* for use of my interview. "Nothing if printed in its entirety," I said, savoring the reversal of roles with his paper. And so it was.

The book was panned in the media, and the publicity revived the threats against my life that had been made when Fairness was launched. Back then someone had hung a dead cat on my barn door in Rehoboth with a sign saying, "This will be your fate." I had immediately moved my wife and child in with the Brown University chaplain. This time the anonymous threats came to my office and to the White House by phone and mail.

Suddenly I found more people routinely in my presence. It wasn't until a newspaper reported, "Surrounded by security men, Korff strode to a limousine," that I realized that those "volunteers"—wholesome, solicitous young men and women—were actually a security detail assigned to me. By whom?

It made me extremely uncomfortable. I felt as if I were being spied on, even as one of the "volunteers" partially blocked an irate lady's hand that struck me on the head in the lobby of the Mayflower.

Dr. Alexander Schindler, a prominent cleric of Reform Judaism, added to the furor by calling me an "apologist for rampant immorality" who "perverts democracy and degrades religion." When newspeople asked my reaction, I promised to pray for him.

13 Mea Culpa

My regard for the President did not extend to some on his staff. It took me far too long to recognize the manipulativeness of those whose primary concern was their own standing in the corridors of power. Because of my naiveté, I seriously wronged two people—Gerald Ford and Bernard Nussbaum, counsel to the House Judiciary Committee. Several White House aides saw Ford as a threat to Nixon's survivability and distrusted his professions of loyalty. One day, in an example of what I now realize was logic-chopping, Pat Buchanan listed one contradiction after another in Ford's defense of Nixon and urged me to ask him the following question during our interview for the paperback: "If you firmly believe, as you profess, in the innocence of President Nixon, why would you then agree to succeed him upon impeachment and conviction, since the vacancy would have occurred, not as a consequence of constitutional law, but as one of felonious malice?"

So I did, and the question took Ford aback. He later provided a written answer—that his oath of office required him to uphold the Constitution and succeed to the presidency. But his embarrassment filled me with regret, though I pursued the matter throughout the interview. The question was unfair and a breach of common decency.

Ford was always cordial with me but not more. For most of our encounters he was in a difficult position, such as the February 18th Fairness gala at the Mayflower, when I introduced him as Vice President, "which office I am hopeful he will retain for the next two years."

I later learned that the White House had asked Ford to attend that event to make him aware of Nixon's popular support and lower his expectations; as one staffer put it, "to keep him in line." I felt duped. There was no cause for deception, which in any case was incompatible with what I felt Fairness stood for.

It was Bill Baroody, special assistant to the President, who got me involved in defaming Nussbaum. Baroody came to my office huffing and puffing one day to tell me of a "subversive knave" who had "infiltrated" the House Judiciary Committee to mastermind the President's impeachment as part of a Nixon phobia that went back to his student days at Columbia College and Harvard Law School. It all appeared quite legitimate.

Baroody handed me a "well-researched" story on "this scoundrel" and urged me to print it in the next Fairness newsletter. I did so and have not ceased to regret it.

First, syndicated columnist John Lofton called to ask for particulars and facts against Nussbaum. I had none except the piece in the newsletter and couldn't identify Baroody as its author because it would link the White House to the discrediting of Judiciary Committee personnel.

I then made a few calls around town but could find no reliable source to substantiate the allegations against Nussbaum. What I found was that he was Phi Beta Kappa at Columbia and highly regarded as an Assistant U.S. Attorney for the Southern District of New York and as a law professor on leave from Columbia.

Among other things, Baroody claimed that Nussbaum had been a member of the Young Socialists League at Columbia and had given speeches and distributed literature on campus defending the Soviet repression of the 1956 Hungarian Revolt.

Nussbaum denied the charges in an August 1st Lofton column, pointing out that in fact he had won a prize for a column in the *Columbia Daily Spectator* praising the Hungarian freedom fighters. Lofton concluded: "Everything alleged [against Nussbaum] is false, except that he is a Senior Associate Counsel on the Judiciary Committee."

I phoned Baroody with the fury of a betrayed lover, and he retreated, putting the blame on Buchanan. He even intimated that the Nussbaum affair might have originated in the Oval Office.

Baroody was more fortunate than most White House aides. If the Republicans lost the White House, he could always sign on with the American Enterprise Institute in Washington, a Baroody family venture. He was subsequently named his father's assistant, but was ultimately deposed by the AEI in an inhouse conflict.

One of Nussbaum's assistants on the Judiciary Committee staff, as it happened, was Hillary Rodham, the future First Lady. At the President's request, I had drawn up profiles on several members of the Judiciary staff, but Miss Rodham was not one of them.

In stark contrast, on the White House staff, was Bruce Herschensohn, whose ethics were as unwavering as his loyalty to the President. His gregarious nature smoothed over many a grievance. Bruce came to the White House from the United States Information Agency, where he had made documentary films, the best known of which was *Years of Lightning, Day of Drums*, about John F. Kennedy's presidency.

UPI reporter Helen Thomas once needled Bruce about his "rabbi-minding role." "Where would you be without Korff?" she asked. "With him as a volunteer," he replied.

Equally stalwart was the Stein family—Herb and Mildred and son Ben—who not only didn't jump ship, they dropped anchor. Herb, straitlaced and composed, was chairman of the President's Council of Economic Advisors. Mildred was gentle of voice and devoid of malice to anyone, friend or foe. Ben's sound judgment and skepticism toward public relations belied his status as a junior White House speechwriter.

14   The Last Stand

On August 5th, I returned from Nashville at the urging of the White House and assumed that the President wanted to see me. But it was Julie who had asked my office to find me. Nixon was in the Lincoln Sitting Room with the transcript of the June 23, 1972, tape, the so-called smoking gun he would release to the media later that afternoon.

David and Julie had a draft of the statement the President was going to issue, admitting that the transcript was "at variance" with previous claims he had made. I urged Julie to insist that her father not issue the statement.

"He's sure you'll understand if he doesn't see you now," she told me when she returned. "He's a little embarrassed about the references he made to Jews on the tape."

Later, when asked by the media about those references, I said they were just a manner of speech and that Nixon's deeds far outweighed them. In that, at least, the B'nai B'rith agreed with me.

I left the White House and went to Fairness headquarters, where a phone call was waiting. Ron Ziegler was on the line: "The President wants to see you tomorrow. But please stop at my office on the way."

When I arrived on August 6th, I was met by Ziegler's aide, Diane Sawyer—wholesome, composed, ever so hospitable, but this time without her trademark "Tell me what you know" greeting. Ziegler started by reminding me of my earlier concern for the President's health and state of mind.

Since May 13th, when I had interviewed him for the paperback, I had seen his demeanor rapidly declining. I had urged several senior staffers, including Ziegler, to ease the pressure on him, to act as interlocutors, to try to prevent or at least cushion the desertion of political allies. I suspected that he wanted to fall ill, to find refuge in incapacitation, and then to reemerge somehow when it was all over.

"You were right then and you're right now," Ziegler said. "He can't take it any more. We've run out of options."

I got the message. "What about Mrs. Nixon?" I asked. "What about Tricia and Julie, especially Julie?"

"Well, you can do much to lessen their resistance," he said.

He meant resistance to resignation, though not once did he use the word. He left that for my meeting with the President in his Executive Office Building quarters. Describing that meeting in his 1978 memoirs, Nixon wrote:

> Steve Bull came in to say that Rabbi Korff was waiting for his appointment. I had asked Ziegler to tell him that I had decided to resign and that he should not try to change my mind. Rabbi Korff summoned his usual eloquence and said that, although he would accept whatever I decided, he felt obligated to say what he thought. "You will be sinning against history if you allow the partisan cabal in Congress and the jackals in the media to force you from office," he said. He spoke with the fire of an Old Testament prophet, but he saw that my mind was made up. He said that if I did resign, I owed it to my supporters to do it with my head high and not just slip away.

My memory of the meeting starts with finding Haig, ashen, sitting at a table in the office by a side door, having shuttled between Nixon and Ford on yet another mission "to iron out some rough edges."

The President threw his arms around me buoyantly. He was much less downcast than his aides. He exuded relief, alternately sitting and standing, and puffing on a little pipe. He had made the decision in stages, followed by a sigh that stayed frozen in his bearing.

"You did quite a job on my family," he said. "I wish you'd dissuade them from pressuring me not to resign."

I expressed my disagreement with his decision, then agreed to do what he asked.

To care is to behold the Divine. To care is to exhilarate when in agony, to cheer when sad, to glow when downcast, to be steady when the ground beneath quakes, to be a fully lighted chandelier in a labyrinth of doubt. To care is to dispel the shadows that would eclipse your sphere. That is how I had hoped to care for Richard Nixon. He should not have departed ignominiously. It had never dawned on me that he would.

I dared not contemplate the outcome for him and found myself making the transition from service to the presidency to servant of the President. Twice I asked him about the jeopardy that resignation might put him in, and he answered with platitudes about what he owed to the American people. But as he walked me to the door, I quietly asked again, "Aren't you concerned about your legal safety after resignation?"

"I'm confident, although the last word will come later today," he said.

At the door, he asked, "What can I do for you while I'm still in office?"

"Nothing, Mr. President," I said. "The opportunity to care is the most rewarding gift you could have given me." Then I had a thought. "You may autograph that photograph," I said, pointing to a two-by-three-foot photograph against the wall showing me presenting him with a copy of *The Personal Nixon: Staying on the Summit.*

Two days later, the photograph arrived at my office, inscribed: "To Rabbi Korff, for whose friendship, support, and wise counsel I shall always be grateful. Richard Nixon, August 8, 1974."

After I left the EOB office, the President, according to his 1978 memoirs, summoned Rose Mary Woods and asked her to tell the Nixon family that he would have to resign. He then "took a yellow pad from the desk." At the top, he says, he wrote "Resignation Speech."

Meanwhile, I went directly from the EOB office to the family quarters and talked with Julie, who accompanied me to the Oval Office, where we thought the President might show up. But he didn't, so we left, Julie returning to the family quarters and I heading straight into the press corps area.

"Unless there is an immediate outpouring of support addressed to the White House," I told the news people there, "it is my opinion and only my opinion he may resign for the national interest."

I then conferred with Othal Brand, Admiral Strauss, and Earl Butz, and we decided to leak the imminence of the resignation, which I judged to be within twenty-four hours. We felt we had much to gain and little to lose. If the outpouring of support that would result did not change the President's mind, it would at least "ease his and his family's grief," as Admiral Strauss put it.

I chose Douglas C. Wilson, chief of the *Providence Journal-Bulletin*'s Washington Bureau, as the leakee, a designation that won him the 1975 Merriman Smith

Award from the White House Correspondents' Association "for excellence in presidential news coverage."

On the tenth anniversary of the resignation, Wilson, now director of publications and editor of a quarterly for Amherst College, told how it happened in a *Journal-Bulletin* article entitled "How Nation Learned Nixon Would Resign":

> As soon as I arrived home from the *Journal-Bulletin's* office . . . at dinnertime on Tuesday, Aug. 6, my wife told me that Rabbi Baruch Korff had just spent an hour with Nixon. The report had come over the radio.
>
> The capital was taut with suspense—would Nixon resign or stay on to fight impeachment over Watergate? For several days, he had seen no one except his family and his closest advisers. But Korff . . . was one of the President's closest confidants. Perhaps I could reach him for an eyewitness story.
>
> I [had] interviewed him, covered his pro-Nixon rallies, and liked him in spite of his extreme opinions. (After one visit with Nixon, Korff insisted that "a thousand Watergates—nay, ten thousand Watergates—are infinitesimal and are not worth one minute of his time.") The rabbi berated the press for trying to "lynch" the President; but because I reported Korff's own sentiments and not what I thought of them, he told me I was not like other reporters. He said I was an oddball: I was fair.
>
> I . . . went to the phone, hoping Korff would tell an oddball like me how the President looked—how he was taking the strain. Korff lived in a Washington hotel that

summer, but I didn't know which one, so I called a dozen hotels asking for "Rabbi Korff's room." . . . Then I dialed the Fairfax, and when I asked for the room, the clerk rang.

No one answered. . . . I finally went to bed without a story.

At 10 o'clock the next morning, Aug. 7, the . . . answering service of the Washington bureau gave me an "urgent" message to call Korff's office. . . . There, an assistant . . . told me that although Korff wasn't speaking to other reporters, he wanted to see me. Fifteen minutes later, I entered the Fairness Committee head-quarters, a little suite of rooms in a shabby building near DuPont Circle.

Normally, the rabbi was lively and sparkling. He would raise his black eyebrows, gesture with a cigar, and make sweeping pronouncements in his strong Ukrainian accent.

This morning he was grave and exhausted. He closed the door, motioned me into a chair, then sat across the room and began to talk slowly. I could barely hear him, so I pulled the chair closer. I started to ask him about his talk with Nixon, but he stopped me by raising his hand.

"I don't believe in leaking," he said almost inaudibly, "but this is imminent. . . ." Then he went on in such a broken and halting manner that I thought he would never finish: "You might want to state that—you have it on the authority—of an undaunted devotee of the President—that—the President—has come to the con-clusion—that the national interest may best be served—

by his resigning—irrespective of the mammoth injustice committed against him—that prompted—this painful decision on his part."

Maybe it was when he came to the words "the national interest may best be served" that I sensed, My God, He's Telling Me Something Important.

Frantically, I began to take notes.

In his memoirs, the President offers this description from the morning of Wednesday, August 7th:

I took the [resignation] speech and started over to the EOB office. As I walked through the West Wing, I heard phones ringing in every office. The switchboard was deluged with calls from people who had stood by me through it all. . . . They were calling to say that I must fight on. That decision, I had to repeat to myself again, was made. Now I did not want to know about these calls.

United Press International reported that "secretaries and volunteers were pressed into service" late into Wednesday evening "to answer a special bank of phones" at the EOB. Elizabeth Drew, in her book *Washington Journal,* says of mid-day August 8th:

One cannot reach the White House by telephone. The switchboard is overloaded. The last time, to my knowledge, that the White House switchboard was overloaded was on that Saturday night when Special Prosecutor Cox was fired.

At Julie's request, I met with the President and his family separately on August 7th and again with the family the next day, to help them deal with the stress of the occasion. From January 1974 through 1978, I participated in two dozen such pastoral sessions with the Nixon family.

15   Abandon Ship

As the end drew near, the advice the President got from political sources was unanimous for resignation. Even Charles Wiggins, one of the President's staunchest supporters on the House Judiciary Committee, told me, after the June 23rd tape was revealed, "Give up. None but the foolhardy would risk self-immolation. Tell him [Nixon] he cannot demand this of his friends. I am now certain of impeachment and conviction." Chuck and his wife Betty were among my dearest friends. I'd been their host on a visit to Israel.

But those who disagreed did not give up. Three visitors to his EOB office mid-day on August 7th were his sons-in-law, Ed Cox and David Eisenhower, and Bruce Herschensohn, the President's memoirs say. All spoke fervently against resignation.

Bruce argued that seventy-five years later, some young person faced with a hopeless duty should be able to say,

"President Nixon didn't give up and neither will I." Needless to say, I found Bruce's presence at my side highly comforting two days later.

Just before his resignation speech to the nation on the night of August 8th, the President met with thirty-four close Congressional friends, fourteen of them Southern Democrats. Among them were three of the four Democratic deans of the Senate—James Eastland and John Stennis of Mississippi and John McClellan of Arkansas.

The fourth dean, Russell Long of Louisiana, was traveling but sent Nixon a letter that ended up at Fairness headquarters. The White House Post Office sent all post-resignation Nixon mail there so it wouldn't be impounded with the other Nixon papers. The President instructed me to open it and send on to him what I felt he should see.

Written on Delta Airlines stationery, Long's letter, which Nixon let me keep, reads in part:

> Somehow Americans don't ever seem to understand some very obvious facts although it is demonstrated before their eyes every day. No one is perfect on this side of heaven, and all of our idols have feet of clay. This earth is a testing place to see whether each of us is worth passing on to something better.
>
> I thank God that you did not force matters to an impeachment trial in the Senate. You knew how I felt about matters, and you could have relied on me, but the nation would have suffered, and I very much feared

that you and your family would have suffered the torment of Hades for no good purpose. Now that the tragic moment is behind us, you will find that a great number of people truly love you, and that number will grow.

Please forgive those who will do and say mean things during the next several months. They are to be pitied. They know no better; we should hope that *they* can be saved.

Carolyn and I are among the millions who genuinely love you, Pat, Tricia, and Julie. Should it ever be necessary, we would gladly carry your cross an extra mile.

Yes, Watergate badly damaged GOP prospects, but I couldn't help wishing that influential Republicans—like Minority Leader Hugh Scott of Pennsylvania and Barry Goldwater of Arizona in the Senate and Minority Leader John Rhodes of Arizona and former member Melvin Laird in the House—had stood by this Republican President as did the four Democratic deans.

I was also disappointed in the Cabinet. After the President assured them on August 6th that he wouldn't resign, one official was quoted describing the assurance as "vintage Nixon." Another said that Nixon was holding out only for "concurrence" on a pardon. Had there been a net, they all would have jumped except for Butz, Simon, and Kissinger. The Cabinet shifted allegiance to Ford without a sign of regret. Only Earl Butz showed genuine emotion.

At the President's moving farewell to the White House

staff in a packed East Room on the morning of August 9th, when finally the tears I'd held back came streaming down my face, one by one the four Nixons onstage steadied their eyes on me as I tried to hide my face.

16   The Pardon

On September 8th, President Ford stirred up the unholy alliance again—and may have cost himself re-election in 1976—by granting Nixon a full and absolute pardon for all offenses he might have committed against the United States during his presidency.

In the previous month, the pro-pardon players had included Al Haig, Henry Kissinger, Nelson and David Rockefeller, speechwriter Ray Price, and Leonard Garment. Nixon's daughters, despairing at their father's physical and emotional deterioration, implored Ford to "act before it's too late." Foremost among the many anti-pardon players was Mel Laird, former Secretary of Defense and Domestic Counselor under Nixon.

Fairness used what was left of its clout with Republicans Scott, Goldwater, Rhodes, Ed Brooke, and more than three dozen other legislators who had come out for impeachment to get them to publicly urge a pardon.

We hoped that would give the new President an out to counter the suspicion that a pardon had been a condition of the resignation.

It was widely understood that after meeting with Nixon on August 7th to urge him to resign, Goldwater, Scott, and Rhodes made sure Ford knew that Nixon was not about to surrender his Oval Office immunity without a solid "understanding" with Ford.

Officially, Ford said he decided on a pardon in early September after learning that Nixon was under investigation for possible criminal activity in ten different matters and that it would be at least nine months before any trial could start. Nixon was told of the pardon on September 4th, Ford said, and a lawyer for the White House then spent two days in California negotiating the disposition of Nixon's papers and tapes and Nixon's statement of "contrition."

But Ford also told a House Judiciary subcommittee in October that Haig had raised both topics with him—resignation and pardon—as early as August 1st.

PART II
Servant of the President

17 Paying the Bills

After the resignation, it seemed wasteful to the Fairness hierarchy to fold the organization we had built. So we created a successor, the United States Citizens' Congress, to promote conservative causes through scholarships and events honoring international leaders and to keep Nixon's legacy alive.

Mindful of George Meany's partisanship, we tried to set a higher standard. In the bimonthly Citizens' Congress newsletter, for example, we gave half a page to Meany's successor, Lane Kirkland, to argue against right-to-work laws after we had carried an article favoring such laws. That decision was controversial among Citizens' Congress members, but Frank Fitzsimmons applauded it.

At the same time we also set up the President Nixon Justice Fund to pay his legal bills. I announced the Fund's formation in Jerusalem, where negotiations on disposing of the Sinai were under way. I was there because of my access to Anwar Sadat.

In four years, the Justice Fund raised and distributed $358,000 to lawyers for defending Nixon against witness subpoenas for trials and civil matters, in endless negotiations over his papers and tapes, and in disbarment proceedings. Most of the money went to the Washington firm of Miller, Cassidy, Larroca & Lewin.

Jack Miller was Nixon's lawyer, but it was Ray Larroca who regularly visited our office seeking payment. In the late fall of 1974, when subpoenas were raining down and Nixon's health was most precarious, I threatened to have the firm fired if it didn't keep him out of court. Larroca promised to adopt delaying tactics. As it turned out, Nixon's only court appearance was a voluntary one in late 1980 as a witness in the trial of two former FBI agents.

Contributions to the Fund came from many sources and were often accompanied by messages. One letter, from W. Peter Mardwede, M.D., of Baltimore, said: "This check [$200] comes from my first month's pay as an intern. I can't think of a better way to put this money to use than to help President Nixon with his legal problems."

A sixty-seven-year-old woman in New York City sent her Social Security check with a request for anonymity and a simple "God bless you!" On the other hand, there was this message with a modest check from a college student in Minneapolis: "I am participating in a smoking control program. Part of this program is to specify someone whom I must contribute money [to] if I don't achieve my smoking goals. I have specified you because it is particularly aversive for me to give you money."

A substantial contribution came from Elizabeth Taylor following a visit to my office from her attorney to explain the circumstances. Julie Eisenhower had told me the background earlier. It seems that Henry Wynberg, Miss Taylor's escort at the time, was asked by a Japanese journalist to arrange an interview with Julie for which she or her favorite charity would receive $25,000. But Wynberg never passed the money on, so Miss Taylor made good, then expressed regret by phone for what had happened.

A frequent source of last resort when Nixon's legal bills were in arrears was Mortimer J. Propp of New York City, a founder of the United Jewish Appeal half a century before, and his wife Enia and brother Seymour. When I was in my late teens, at the behest of the saintly Dr. Leo Jung of Yeshiva College in New York City, I had taught the three sons of the late Morris Propp—Mortimer, Seymour, and Ephraim—a tractate of the Talmud to commemorate their father's name.

I found it far more difficult to raise money for the Justice Fund than I had for Fairness. Many Fairness backers had been motivated by opposition to the liberalism of Nixon's opponents or by concern for the presidency, not by Nixon himself. Legal fees were irrelevant to these rationales. Others had thought Nixon personally innocent and perhaps felt betrayed by the June 23rd tape. Most had modest resources to start with and had no interest in depleting them further to benefit lawyers they doubtless considered overpaid.

I obtained a number of donations on the condition that they would be tax-exempt. They would be if the issues being litigated were constitutional, and Nixon thought all the issues were. But the legal advice I was given in 1975—by Webster, Kilcullen & Chamberlain in Washington via Miller, Cassidy—said that some were, others were doubtful, and exempt funds had to be kept segregated from the rest. I managed to retain most of these donations but had to return a few thousand dollars.

Concerned about anonymity, some foreign sources I appealed to shied from association with the Justice Fund. I told them to find whatever route they were comfortable with that could accommodate both their concern and mine. I wasn't privy to how all of them proceeded, but some contacted Nixon directly, and he periodically augmented our payments to the lawyers.

Publisher Walter Annenberg preferred to place Nixon on an annual retainer of $75,000, for which I was grateful. Because Nixon was disbarred in California and New York, the retainer could not be for legal services, so it became a consultancy. He advised Annenberg on his new publication *American Views*. Only two issues ever appeared, but Nixon stayed on the payroll.

18   The Jewish Response

A high-profile Israeli who preferred anonymity made a substantial donation to the Justice Fund. This donor had earlier encouraged me to "go forward" with my plans to defend the presidency, saying, "I am obliged to share your forebodings. We should have balance [among U.S. Jews]. Your sentiments are mine exactly."

Later, I pleaded for permission to reveal this donor's name in hopes of countering those American Jews who were condemning me as a traitor to the Jewish people. But I was held to my commitment.

In general, the Orthodox rabbinate in the United States whispered their support for my defense of Nixon, and the Reform and Conservative branches were either silent or outspokenly critical. Two who ignored the fallout and backed me publicly were Dr. Jakob Petuchowski of Hebrew Union College (Reform) and

Dr. Seymour Siegel of the Jewish Theological Seminary (Conservative).

Most of the Jewish weeklies, subsidized by philanthropies commited to Israel, were not even remotely interested in inquiring why the Israeli media were largely supportive of my efforts. A columnist in the *Jewish Floridian* ended a long diatribe this way: "Let me commend to Rabbis Korff, Seymour Siegel, and Jakob Petuchowski this Psalm which reads in part: 'How long will you judge unjustly and show favor to the wicked?'"

One weekly not part of the posse pursuing me was the *Wisconsin Jewish Chronicle* and its editor, Paul F. Levy—small in circulation but large on wisdom.

In August 1974, I received an invitation from the Roger Williams Lodge of B'nai B'rith in Providence, to which I belonged, inviting me to address the members. After a date was agreed on and a second lodge included and notices were sent out, all hell broke loose. "Korff's appearance will cost you membership," the parent organization warned.

The embarrassed lodge president, attorney Mitchell S. Riffkin, canceled the lecture. To think that Roger Williams founded Providence in 1636 as a haven for the persecuted!

More than a year after Nixon's resignation, I dined with John Mitchell, Nixon's first-term Attorney-General, at the Jockey Club in Washington's Fairfax Hotel, where I maintained a small apartment. I was bemoaning the criticism from my own people, and Mitchell said, "I'm not surprised. The Anti-Defamation League has been an informant for the FBI a good many years—compiling dossiers on Jews in the arts and Hollywood for Hoover."

I was stunned and sickened. Shades of the *Judenrat*!

Mitchell also pointed out, however, that at times the ADL was a valuable ally of the FBI, particularly in investigations of antisemitism and terrorism. The FBI subsidized some of those collaborations, he said.

Turndowns came from non-Jews as well, of course, as the 1978 dedication in Hyden, Kentucky, demonstrated (see below, p. 130).

One precaution I took because of the threats I received was having two apartments, one at the Mayflower, one at the Fairfax. In late 1977, I was dining at the Mayflower with Jack Kahn and his son and daughter-in-law when a hotel official rushed up to tell me I had a phone call.

Rebecca and I had recently been divorced, and Zamira, then ten, was staying with a governess in an apartment next door to the Fairfax. It seems that two young, olive-skinned men had entered the apartment building's elevator with Zamira and the governess and stopped it between floors. The men spoke English to the females and Arabic to each other, not realizing that the governess spoke Arabic as well.

When the elevator finally reached a floor, FBI agents, who had been keeping an eye on my family because of the threats, were right there and took the men into custody. One was Iraqi, the other Jordanian, and both were illegal aliens. But I never got the whole story. All the FBI would tell me was, "We're handling it, rabbi, don't worry."

I thought perhaps the men were only trying to chat up the governess, a former Miss Jerusalem who was handpicked for Zamira by Israeli security. But the governess, who had some connection to intelligence work, thought it had been a kidnap attempt.

19   Recovery and Loss

At Casa Pacifica a week after the pardon, Nixon mentioned that Ron Ziegler had been urging him to lay out the whole truth, including the questionable schemes by people he trusted, because the facts were less incriminating than the conjectures flooding the country. Nixon's statement of "contrition" when the pardon was announced had said only, "I was wrong in not acting more decisively and more forthrightly in dealing with Watergate."

I told him it was too late. It would only fuel the fires again and gain him few converts. "Had you laid bare the facts in their entirety instead of piecemeal prior to or during the Ervin hearings," I said, "you might have gotten away with censure. To admit now to obstruction of justice after a pardon might even jeopardize your emoluments. God knows what else it would lead to. Leave well enough alone."

Anguish filled his eyes. He leaned forward to rub his left leg, which was resting on an ottoman.

I was particularly concerned that Nixon's personal recovery, as well as his eventual public reemergence, might be inhibited by an outright admission of guilt, both to himself and to the public. "I can't picture you," I told him, alluding to his card-playing in the Navy, "the best poker player throwing in his hand!"

Ziegler, a protegé of Nixon's former chief of staff, H. R. Haldeman, from their J. Walter Thompson days in advertising, proved to be a surprisingly helpful aide and sounding board for Nixon out of office. No one was able to char his asbestos skin, not John Connally, the former Treasury Secretary, who was a Nixon favorite, or Melvin Laird, both of whom wanted him fired. Nor Nixon confidant Charles "Bebe" Rebozo, who told one reporter, "Ron Ziegler is a nice young man but he doesn't know public relations."

Ziegler, who had not been touched by Watergate, was discreet and loyal. Once, at Casa Pacifica, his assistant, Diane Sawyer, interrupted to say, "He wants you." Jerking his body in annoyance, Ziegler responded, "Let him wait." We were watching Gerald Ford address Congress for the first time as President. After a few minutes of self-assertion, Ziegler left to see Nixon, who was also watching his successor.

Throughout the fall of 1974, Ziegler came into his own. Nixon had been admitted to Long Beach Memorial Hospital for blood clots, and Ziegler developed the confidence of a son who is suddenly thrust into independent decision-making. Throughout Nixon's surgery and incapacity, Ziegler acquitted himself well with the media, while I worked the Fairness grapevine to get tens of thousands of letters of encouragement sent to the patient.

Personally, I found Ziegler forthright, caring, thoughtful, and dedicated. He was totally dependent on Nixon's fortunes. He had no independent resources, either professional or financial, to fall back on.

During November and early December of 1974, I shuttled to and from Boston to be at the bedside of my ailing brother, Samuel. He was only two years older than I, but he was my mentor. As head of the Va'ad Harabanim and the Associated Synagogues of Massachusetts and presiding justice of the Massachusetts Rabbinic Court, he was a worthy heir to our father, who had been Grand Rabbi of Massachusetts for four decades. Samuel carried on the family legacy of seventy-two consecutive rabbinic generations with distinction.

He passed away the last day of Chanukah in December, and the lights of the Jewish community he had served for thirty-six years were dimmed. The Nixons wired their condolences, and a letter dated the same day followed:

> . . . Over the past months, you have given exceptional support to me, both personally and as President. You have stood by me in a difficult time. Even now, as

ever-increasing legal fees confront me, you have moved to assist in defraying the mounting financial burden. . . .

I have heard the proverb that true friends multiply your joy and divide your sorrows. I want to say that thinking of that phrase now, brings you to mind. . . . Our prayers are with you at this time of sorrow. . . .

Of the many thank-you letters I received from Richard Nixon over the years, this is the one I value most.

Although immersed in the observance of shiva, the traditional mourning period, I continued to make previously scheduled appearances for the Justice Fund. Unlike those who tend to secularize the spiritual, I prefer to spiritualize the secular. Both life and death are spiritual journeys.

20 Candor in California

On Nixon's sixty-second birthday, January 9, 1975, I met with the media at the San Clemente Inn at his urging. A *Los Angeles Times* reporter said that he had a "few embarrassing questions" for me.

Was it true that I had been detained in a French prison in 1947 for attempting to bomb England by air? I said yes.

What was the disposition of the case? I was found not guilty, I replied, but I was guilty and pleaded so.

At the time I was protesting Britain's refusal to allow the *Exodus–1947* to land its human cargo in Palestine. My colleagues and I had two homemade bombs and wanted to make the world aware of our determination. But at the behest of Congressman McCormack—and probably to the relief of the British government—Secretary of State George Marshall intervened.

Was it true that I had been a member of the Stern gang, the reporter asked. I said yes.

Technically, I had been part of the Irgun's liaison team with the Sternists, whom I broke with over their 1948 assassination of U.N. mediator Folke Bernadotte. At the time I told Yitzhak Shamir that the murder was morally indefensible and stupid. He disclaimed personal responsibility.

The press conference pleased Nixon, who had asked that it be taped.

In February, when the six-month transition allowance ended, Nixon's staff was drastically reduced. They held a going-away party at the San Clemente Inn. As I was on my way down a corridor, a member of the ever-present press shouted at me, asking what I knew about the 18-minute gap in the tape of June 20, 1972. I said, truthfully, that I didn't know anything about it.

Rose Mary Woods heard the exchange and came up to me at the party. "Didn't he tell you?" she asked.

"Tell me what?" I said.

"We both did it," she said with a laugh, then added, "accidentally."

"Of course," I said.

Court-appointed technicians had said that the gap was caused by at least five manual erasures. Rose Mary told me that Haldeman, several months after he resigned, had called the President's attention to the June 20th tape with a warning phone call.

As some of the Fairness faithful who went supper-clubbing during the five-day convention discovered, comedian Mark Russell commemorated Rose Mary's role in the tape gap episode: "If Rose Mary Woods had been Moses' secretary, we would have only three Commandments."

The mood at the going-away party was depressing, uncertainty punctuated by occasional bursts of anger. Some people asked me for help in getting jobs or for money to tide them over until they got jobs. "Have a drink, it's not a wake!" someone shouted.

Ziegler hinted that he needed plane fare for the return East of his family, which had stayed in Virginia for most of the transition period but was visiting at Nixon's suggestion. I had the Citizens' Congress remit $4,000 to him. (The check was earmarked "for services to, and at the direction of, President Nixon," who was considered an ex-officio member of the Congress.)

When told of this, Nixon expressed reservations. "Ron doesn't know how to manage his money," he said.

Around that time I gave an interview to the press that angered Nixon. I described him as having "profound regrets" and said he "agonizes" and is "tormented," in poor "physical and emotional health," and given to "depression."

"Do you want to make an invalid out of me?" he asked.

"I've got to describe what I see," I said.

"But you're a diplomat," he said. "You know I have enemies."

I was usually able to bring him out of his dark moods. In my travels people would occasionally give me things for him. An 1890 bottle of wine from a Rothschild vineyard was one gift. A silver snuffbox that had been a family heirloom was another. Sometimes it was a letter that the writer wanted to make sure he saw. There were gifts for Mrs. Nixon too.

So when I showed up, whatever his mood Nixon would often smile and ask, "More goodies?" Indeed, this most reserved of men would usually embrace me, perhaps because I was several inches shorter than he. But that was not his greeting when I had done something he didn't like, when I was the target of the dark mood.

21 A Real First Lady

Patricia Nixon was probably the most heroic of the Nixon quartet. Her husband gave her more exposure to the world arena and more accolades than she ever wanted. During Watergate she wanted to escape to find peace and solace, but outwardly she urged her husband not to give up, not to resign. Her encouragement was another way of saying, "You're right. You're innocent."

There was so much I wanted to do for her, but she was less accessible than her husband, and I shied away from attracting attention to her grief. The punishment she absorbed was solely deflective of her husband's and more unfair for that.

I got to know her somewhat better at Casa Pacifica. She was not cold and distant, as some would have us believe. She was a loving, pulsating, compassionate soul.

In that first year out of office, when the family's finances were often in the red, I sent her a sizable birthday gift. She returned it with a request that it go to the Justice Fund:

> You, Rebecca, and Zamira were ever so kind to send me the generous check as a birthday surprise. It brought joy to the day and happy thoughts of your treasured friendship. Having endorsed it for the Justice Fund, I am enclosing it in this note along with a postal money order which was received from another friend.

On a visit shortly thereafter, I arranged for roses to be delivered to her every week. She was away, I believe, visiting the children. I had to go on to Los Angeles and then to Washington. There I found another handwritten note:

> I was deeply disappointed to have missed your visit to San Clemente and now look forward to the "next time." Lois Gaunt has told me of your kindness in wanting us to have a weekly bouquet of roses. What a thoughtful person you are to plan such a delightful surprise! With constant appreciation for your many kindnesses over the years . . .

More than anyone else, she was responsible for the rehabilitation of Richard Nixon. King Solomon, the author of the biblical Book of Proverbs, must have modeled his "woman of valor" on an ancient prototype of Pat Nixon: "Many daughters have done worthily, but thou excellest them all."

Nixon got a chance to return the favor when Mrs. Nixon had a stroke in July 1976 after reading *The Final Days*, with its scurrilous allegations about Nixon-family drinking problems and worse. He made the 80-mile round trip to the hospital daily for the first two weeks of her stay, selected the mail to bring her from the million-plus letters she received, and fussed over her with flowers and encouragement.

While Julie was more like their father, Tricia was more like Mrs. Nixon. She and Ed Cox lived in New York City, not Washington, so I didn't get to know her as well as I did the rest of the family. I found Tricia warm and affectionate, if less demonstrative than her sister. I was grateful that she seemed at ease with me on the seven or eight times our paths crossed.

22   A False Step

In March of 1975 I tried to help line up a paid television interview for Nixon. The idea, which neither his doctor nor his lawyers liked, came from Nixon himself through Paul Presley, owner of the San Clemente Inn, and Johnny Grant, a local TV personality. CBS had paid Haldeman $100,000 for an interview, so we asked $250,000.

But the networks weren't interested. Haldeman had been anything but forthcoming during his interview, and CBS had been roundly criticized for "checkbook journalism." I turned to David Susskind, who'd had me on his TV show many times even though he disliked Nixon. But he had no luck with his contacts either.

When I sought his help, Susskind's first response was: "How long are you going to stay with that deadbeat?" After my pitch for the Justice Fund on one show, he asked me on the air with a smile, "Do you really expect my viewers to contribute to Richard Nixon?" Oddly enough after one of my appearances on the Susskind Show I discovered an envelope stuffed with $1800 in twenty dollar bills at my door at the Fairfax Hotel with a note saying "Susskind was wrong".

Nixon did not get on TV until 1977, four 90-minute shows on David Frost's syndicated program. The price: $600,000 and 20 percent of the profits. Hollywood agent Swifty Lazar brokered the deal, as he had the sale of Nixon's memoirs for $2 million.

If Haldeman had been the inspiration for the Nixon-Frost interviews, he was also their casualty. He watched them from Lompoc Federal Prison in California, where he was serving eighteen months for his role in Watergate. Nixon portrayed himself as an innocent done in by loyalty to overzealous subordinates like Haldeman. He also revealed that certain phrases Haldeman had found moving face-to-face were rhetoric used to manipulate others as well.

So Haldeman wrote his account of Watergate, *The Ends of Power*. He charged that Nixon had orchestrated the coverup, authorized the Watergate burglaries, probably erased the missing 18- minutes of tape, and specifically ordered the break-in at the office of the psychiatrist for Daniel Ellsberg, the man accused of leaking the Pentagon Papers in 1971. Once reconciled with Nixon after his release, however, Haldeman repudiated the book, blaming his co-author.

In late May and early June 1975, I was to give five lectures in New England—two at commencements, two on the Middle East, and one of a religious nature. All had been scheduled eighteen months previously, but all were canceled within a few days of each other in May. I didn't think that was a coincidence.

Disgusted and concerned about my livelihood, I told Admiral Strauss, "I'm over my head," and announced my resignation as head of the Justice Fund. Nixon expressed regret and the hope I would reconsider.

I specified my reasons as personal and financial hardship to the media. But in a follow-up interview with Jules Witcover of the *Washington Post*, my careless choice of words in explaining the Watergate coverup from Nixon's point of view made it seem that he had admitted his role in it to me. The June 23rd tape may have confirmed that role, but Nixon had never admitted it to the nation or to me.

The result was more headlines and a phone call from Nixon, who was furious. I flew out to California and we patched things up. With the promise of help from Ken Khachigian, one of the best assets salvaged from the White House staff, I also changed my mind about stepping down.

Using the Casa Pacifica phones, I lined up a hundred loyalists in the Los Angeles area to reinvigorate the Fund. Stalwarts who had become friends—such as Cynthia Preiss of Glendale, Diane and Alfred Jacobs of Beverly Hills, and the Baldwins—came through once more and dispelled any reservations I had. Nixon followed with a letter on June 18th:

> . . . I am asking you the personal favor that you consider postponing your plans to resign while the

Board of Trustees continues their search for . . . a suitable successor. . . .

You have already done so much that I hesitate to ask you to do more. But I hope that you will accept this personal request to continue for at least a while longer.

The "while longer" lasted another sixteen months, when family problems required me to step down. And in December of 1978, Lloyd R. Johnson, a nursing-home owner from Ann Arbor, Michigan, who had succeeded me as presiding trustee of the President Nixon Justice Fund, announced the Fund's dissolution. At San Clemente the previous May, Nixon had told Johnson, "I am now in a financial position to assume this responsibility."

23 The Yom Kippur War

One day in June 1975, Nixon reminisced about "a desperate phone call" from the Israeli Prime Minister during the Yom Kippur War, in October 1973. He had taken the call in Key Biscayne, Florida.

"Golda Meir spoke," he said, "as if she were dying: 'We have lost one third of our air force, one third of our armor, and 1,000 men to Soviet surface-to-air missiles.' She also alluded to possible deployment of 'uncommon weapons' unless her Air Force was immediately replenished. I knew what she meant and the consequences that would follow, particularly between the Soviet Union and ourselves.

"I acted quickly despite the resistance of [Secretary of Defense James] Schlesinger, who claimed that an airlift of such proportions would alarm the Arabs and the entire Moslem world and get the Soviets even more involved. He also vigorously resisted the depletion of our air reserve.

"Henry Kissinger waited to be goaded by me. My instructions to him before Mrs. Meir's call were that he talk to the Germans about refueling rights. Henry said the Germans were stubborn. They said they couldn't risk a cutoff of their oil supply."

Nixon's words came in torrents. "Portugal [the Azores] was reluctant and finally relented. I allayed Schlesinger's fears and ordered immediate compliance with Israel's request on a scale exceeding the Berlin airlift—C-5s, Phantoms, surface-to-air missiles, electronic jamming, and advanced equipment we ourselves had not tested in combat. We kept our promise, and without our help Israel might have gone down the tubes."

It was the first time he had discussed the Yom Kippur War with me in detail. I was awed by his account—and disgusted anew with Nixon's critics. Some of them called to mind the fellow who declined to be saved from drowning because he disapproved of his rescuer's credentials. During her call to Key Biscayne, Golda Meir had reminded Nixon of the 100,000 Americans living in Israel "who are in imminent peril."

In her 1975 book *My Life,* after saying "there is still a great deal that cannot be told" about the Yom Kippur War, Mrs. Meir mentioned a call she made to Simcha Dinitz, Israel's ambassador to Washington:

I remember calling him once at 3 a.m., Washington time, and he said, "I can't speak to anyone now, Golda. It is much too early." . . . I knew that President Nixon had promised to help us, and I knew from my past experience with him that he would not let us down. Let me, at this point, repeat something that I have said often before (usually to the extreme annoyance of many of my American friends). However history judges Richard Nixon—and it is probable that the verdict will be very harsh—it must also be put on the record forever that he did not break a single one of the promises he made to us.

She continues: "So why was there a delay? 'I don't care what time it is,' I raged at Dinitz. 'Call Kissinger now. In the middle of the night. We need the help today because tomorrow it may be too late.'" That was when the phone rang at Key Biscayne. Mrs. Meir's narrative resumes:

The story has already been published of that delay, of the U.S. Defense Department's initial reluctance to send military supplies to us in U.S. planes and of the problems that arose when we feverishly shopped around for other planes—when all the time huge transports of Soviet aid were being brought by sea and air to Egypt and Syria and we were losing aircraft at a disturbing rate (not in air battles but to the Soviet missiles on both fronts). Each hour of waiting that passed was like a century to me, but there was no alternative other than to hold on tight and hope that the next hour would bring better news.   I phoned Dinitz and told him that I was ready to fly to Washington incognito to meet with Nixon if he thought it could be arranged. "Find out immediately," I said, "I want to go as soon as possible." But it wasn't necessary. At last Nixon himself ordered the giant C-5 Galaxies to be sent, and the first flight arrived on the ninth day of the war. On October 14 the airlift was invaluable. It not only lifted our spirits, but also served to make the American position clear to the Soviet Union, and it undoubtedly served to make our victory possible. When I heard that the planes had touched down in Lydda, I cried for the first time since the war had begun, though not for the last. That was also the day on which we published the first casualty list—656 Israelis had already died in battle.

But even the Galaxies that brought us tanks, ammunition, clothing, medical supplies and air-to-air rockets couldn't bring all that was required. What about the planes? The Phantoms and the Skyhawks had to be refueled en route, so they were refueled in the air. But they came—and so did the Galaxies that landed in Lydda, sometimes at the rate of one every fifteen minutes.

Within two weeks after the hostilities broke out, Nixon told me, Aleksei Kosygin appeared in Cairo and Damascus to assess the damage and negotiate expansion of Soviet involvement. Intelligence reported Soviet airborne divisions and "85 Soviet ships, including landing craft and ships carrying troop helicopters in the Mediterranean."

Top aides were quickly assembled—"Kissinger, Haig, Schlesinger, Scowcroft, Moorer, and Director Colby of the CIA. . . . Their unanimous recommendation was that we should put all American conventional and nuclear forces on military alert." That was done, and the Soviets backed off. Mrs. Meir adds:

> The story of the subsequent U.S. alert is not for me to tell. There is only one thing that I wish to say about it. I know that in the United States at that time many people assumed that the alert was "invented" by President Nixon in order to divert attention from the Watergate problem, but I didn't believe that then, and I do not believe it now.

After the Yom Kippur War, I gained the attention of Ambassador Dinitz. He frequented my apartment at the Mayflower for lunch or just to chat—never idly, always to probe—and to remind me that my access to the White House was "invaluable" and "crucial" to Israel's interests.

I once took pity on his security escort, walking the corridor outside my door, and offered to obtain a chair and refreshments for him. Dinitz demurred. "That's his job," he said.

On occasion, I would suggest that we meet at the Israeli embassy, but Dinitz did not take up the offer. He never invited me to any official embassy function, which almost always included Nixon's bitterest detractors and therefore mine. He said as much by way of apology: "I don't want to see you hurt."

He expressed sympathy with my "unenviable" role as "defender of Richard Nixon even when it puts you at odds with the liberal supporters of Israel. Israel needs both." Ironically, because of my activities overseas I was frequently a guest of a number of ambassadors in Washington, particularly those of Egypt, Iran, and Pakistan.

During the 1974 Sinai negotiations, I had friends on both sides of the conflict, and on a few occasions Dinitz and I found ourselves on the same El Al flight. He would speculate with me on the reasons for my "shuttling habits."

Yitzhak Rabin, hero of the 1967 war, succeeded Golda Meir as Israel's Prime Minister, and Nixon mentioned one day that Rabin had been his favorite ambassador. Then he added, "You know, he doesn't look Jewish." I took the bait, assuring him that not all Jews look Jewish and not all the Jewish-looking are Jews.

At my request, Rabin encouraged the purchase of Nixon's Key Biscayne residence by private interests. Nixon had asked me in 1975 to help Bebe Rebozo set up a group to acquire the property for historical purposes. But the plan never took root, and interest shifted to Nixon's birthplace in Yorba Linda, California, which was acquired in February 1978 for $125,000.

The Nixon library, which cost $25 million and opened in 1990, is on the Yorba Linda site. Like all presidential libraries, it was built by private funds. Bill Simon chaired the fund-raising effort. Unlike other presidential libraries, however, it is maintained by private funds, access to its documents remaining under the Nixon family's control.

Accordingly, it is not considered a presidential library under the 1955 Presidential Libraries Law—the only one of the ten repositories of the effects of former Presidents that isn't. By act of Congress, the National Archives still has Nixon's White House tapes, as well as the Nixon papers that were not shipped to California immediately after his resignation.

The mutual respect between Rabin and Nixon endured. As recently as November 1993, they met at the Stanhope Hotel in Manhattan. Again wearing the mantle of Prime Minister, Rabin had just visited with President Clinton to complete a $2 billion deal for twenty high-tech aircraft specially tailored for Israel.

The F-15E was designed for long-range ground attack and air-to-air combat. Its acquisition signaled a shift in Israeli strategic planning from interception and attack on its closest neighbors—especially Syria, with which peace is a foregone conclusion—to longer-range targets like Iran, Iraq, and Libya. Rabin filled Nixon in on the transaction.

24 Don Quixote in K.C.

One of the people I became closest to in the Nixon Cabinet was Bill Simon, Secretary of the Treasury. I enjoyed his sometimes cavalier Alsatian personality and was particularly fond of his wife, Carol, a devout Catholic. On his cue, I involved Gabriele Pendleton of Bryn Athyn, Pennsylvania, Admiral Strauss, and Mortimer Propp in a plan to get Simon nominated as Ford's running mate at the 1976 Republican Convention in Kansas City.

Ford, however, preferred Senator Robert Dole of Kansas, whom he considered a stronger ally in turning back the presidential aspirations of Ronald Reagan. He advised Simon in no uncertain terms to discourage a draft.

For his part, Simon, an investment banker, knew that his lack of elective office was a handicap to a political future and set out to become better known by accepting every speaking opportunity and joining the Citizens' Congress.

I intended to talk up Simon's candidacy at the convention anyway, but my real reason for going was to make sure Richard Nixon was not forgotten. "I hope you're going to the convention," he had said to me. "I hope you'll do your best to make them aware of my exile."

But his name and likeness were nowhere to be found on literature or poster at Kansas City. I sought the help of delegates angered by this development in an attempt to get invited to address the convention. To that end, I attended several receptions in the Kansas City area in the forty-eight hours preceding the convention.

R. Hugh Uhlmann and his gracious wife, Ellen Jane, opened their mansion in Shawnee Mission, Kansas, to me for a reception on Sunday, August 15th. I found myself competing with Monets, Rembrandts, van Goghs, and other masterworks. Columnist Mike Royko of the *Chicago Daily News* was there:

> Baruch Korff, who is Nixon's favorite rabbi, as well as a genuine spellbinder, was in splendid form. . . . He sounded like a Biblical prophet, railing against hypocrisy and ingratitude, except that at the moment he was standing in the drawing room of a huge mansion, wearing a tailor-made suit, and holding a pipe. . . .
>
> "I have seen segments of the Republican platform," his voice thundered. "They speak of making the transition from the Bay of Pigs to détente.

"But . . . there is no NAME! It is as if a phantom accomplished it!" . . .

Korff wants the delegates to get up on prime-time TV and become sentimental about what a great guy Nixon was. Korff told the drawing-room crowd: "We are wrong to cover up the salvation of America by Richard Nixon!" . . .

And I suppose Korff has a point. Only four years ago, Nixon was Mr. Big, and many of these same delegates almost swooned as they nominated him for a second term.

Now you can't even find his name scribbled on the wall of a public john.

Volunteers led by the indomitable Gabriele Pitcairn Pendleton—wife of the Swedenborgian bishop of Pennsylvania and one of the Pittsburgh Plate Glass Pitcairns—filled every corridor of the giant Kemper Arena with reminders of Richard Nixon. Leaflets, newsletters, brochures, and pictures of Nixon—banned inside, where the sessions were held—were distributed by sympathetic Republicans.

Some delegates surrendered their accreditation badges to give us greater maneuverability. We invaded committee meetings but in the end were considered saboteurs. Not one speaker had the courage to mention the six years of the Nixon presidency.

The more Nixon was ignored, the more I persisted. Finally a delegate from Puerto Rico agreed to put my name forward to address the convention. Six others pledged to speak for the motion, and 200 delegates promised that if it came to a vote, they would support my right to speak.

As I awaited my big moment on the convention floor, Tom Brokaw of NBC approached for an interview. After it was over, Mike Wallace of CBS was walking my way along a corridor and I heard him mutter into his head-set, "Korff is coming. Should I interview him?" But he passed by.

My interview with Brokaw was the last straw for the convention authorities, who sent security people to examine my credentials and exercised their control of the chair to squelch my bid for good. Here is the way columnist Bill Frank of the *Wilmington Morning News* saw it:

"You loved him once, not without cause. What cause withholds you now to mourn for him?"—Antony's oration in Shakespeare's *Julius Caesar*.

Rabbi Baruch Korff asked to address the Republican National Convention in Kansas City. As I write this column, I doubt if he will get that opportunity. It [is] obvious that no one even want[s] to whisper the name of the man once adored by the Republican Party.

But if Korff should get the opportunity to address the convention, I am sure there would not be all [the] idle chatter on the floor that has been so evident even when the remaining respectables of the Republican Party declaim their platitudes. For Korff is an unequaled spellbinder, particularly on the subject of Richard Nixon.

I met Korff two years ago when he was the guest of Irene McConnell near Wilmington. That was when Korff was invited to speak on behalf of his then new organization, the United States Citizens' Congress.

I arrived at a luncheon determined not to like him, but after a press conference he held and his speech before a sparse audience in the Springer Junior High School, I developed a warm spot in my heart for Korff, though I disagreed with his arguments in behalf of Nixon. . . . I felt [he] was the rare kind of friend a man needs in a time of deepest trouble. . . . [W]e all know only too well what has happened within [the] past four years. And so here we have had the Republican Party diligently avoiding any mention of you know who. All except Baruch Korff.

Mike Royko wrote a column the other day about a meeting Korff had in a huge mansion addressing "about 200 well-heeled Republicans." Korff was quoted as having said: "If the Democrats can let a draft-dodger speak [Arkansas Governor Bill Clinton], why can't a small-town rabbi speak to the Republicans?" Of course Korff knows why. Royko observed that "a fiery Korff speech about the greatness of Nixon could be one of the most memorable moments of this convention." It would top the great speech written by Will Shakespeare and attributed to Marc Antony over the bier of the fallen Caesar, except that I figure Korff would be more sincere than Antony. . . .

Like Antony, he would ask the delegates and Republicans assembled in front of their television screens throughout the nation to remember how they, too, once loved the dethroned president. "But yesterday,"

LA CASA PACIFICA
SAN CLEMENTE, CALIFORNIA

December 18, 1974

Rabbi Baruch Korff
351 Winthrop Street
Rehoboth, Massachusetts 02769

Dear Rabbi Korff:

My gratitude for what you have done in my behalf is not simply seasonal; it is as unvarying as your firm and steady friendship. However, in this special month before the New Year, I did want to take the opportunity to tell you once again how much your loyalty and concern have meant to me.

Over the past months, you have given exceptional support to me, both personally and as President. You have stood by me in a difficult time. Even now, as ever-increasing legal fees confront me, you have moved to assist in defraying the mounting financial burden. For all these things, I will be forever grateful.

I have heard the proverb that true friends multiply your joy and divide your sorrows. I want to say that thinking of that phrase now, brings you to mind.

Best wishes to you for a New Year filled with peace and happiness, and, again, my deepest appreciation for all you have done.

Sincerely,

Richard M. Nixon

Our prayers are with you at this time of sorrow after your brother's death.

New Year's greetings and expression of condolence on the death of his brother from Nixon to Korff, Dec. 18, 1974.

LA CASA PACIFICA
SAN CLEMENTE, CALIFORNIA

April 30, 1975

Dear Rabbi Korff:

I have just learned from Jack Miller's
office that you have made another payment
of $20,000 from the President Nixon Justice
Fund to apply on our legal fees.

For your willingness to undertake what I
know has been a difficult task, and then to
pursue it with such diligence and fidelity,
I shall always be grateful.

Never could I pay you adequately for all you
have done on my behalf. I can only say,
again -- thank you from the bottom of my
heart, and God bless you.

Sincerely,

[signature]

Rabbi Baruch Korff
1221 Connecticut Avenue, N.W.
Washington, D.C. 20036

Letter from Nixon thanking Korff for the funds raised by the President Nixon Justice Fund, April 30, 1975.

June 18, 1975

Dear Rabbi Korff:

Over the past years, your service to the U.S.
Citizens Congress and the President Nixon
Justice Fund have been an inspiration to me
and to the millions of Americans who support
the cause of the Presidency.

Now I am asking you the personal favor that
you consider postponing your plans to resign
while the Board of Trustees continues with
their search for someone to follow you. Your
dynamic leadership and your wise counsel are
more than ever necessary until a suitable
successor can be found.

I shall never be able adequately to express
my deep gratitude for your friendship and support
over these troubled years.

You have already done so much that I hesitate
to ask you to do still more. But I hope that
you will accept this personal request to continue for at least a while longer.

Sincerely,

Rabbi Baruch Korff
U. S. Citizens Congress
1221 Connecticut Avenue, N.W.
Washington, D. C.   20036

Letter from Nixon asking Korff not to resign from the board of trustees of the U.S. Citizens Congress, June 18, 1975.

RICHARD NIXON

LA CASA PACIFICA
SAN CLEMENTE, CALIFORNI

July 16, 1975

Personal and Confidential

Dear Mr. Prime Minister:

I have just had the privilege of seeing our mutual
friend, Rabbi Baruch Korff, when he visited me
here at San Clemente.

He told me of the very kind remarks you made with
regard to the support that I gave to Israel, during
the years that I served in the White House. I want
you to know how deeply grateful I am for your
expressions of continued friendship, despite some
of the difficult problems with which I have been
confronted in recent months. I shall always treasure
the memories I have of those years we worked together
from the time I first met you in 1967 at the conclusion of the war in which the Israeli forces, under
your brilliant leadership, won such a great victory.

You can be sure too that the silver plaque, which
Rabbi Korff told me represents a "Priestly Blessing",
will always have an honored place in our home.

May I also take this opportunity to express my
deepest appreciation for the courtesies you extended
to Rabbi Korff on the occasion of his recent visit
to Jerusalem and, particularly, for your cooperation
in helping us to maintain, as historical monuments,
those places where I have made some of the most
important decisions of my Presidency. In fact, you
will be interested to know that I was at my Key
Biscayne home, in Florida, when the Yom Kippur War

*Letter praising Korff from Nixon to Prime Minister Rabin of Israel,
July 16, 1975.*

began. It was from there that I issued the first
orders calling for the massive airlift, which Israel
so desperately needed in order to meet the threat
to its existence, which was presented because of
the Soviet airlift to the opposing forces.

Rabbi Korff informed me of the very generous cooperation he was receiving from the Israel Torah
Research Institution. I know this would not have been
possible without the personal interest which I understand you expressed in our project.

Mrs. Nixon joins me in extending our very best
wishes to you and Mrs. Rabin during what I know
is a very difficult period for your government and
your country. We look forward to the time when we
shall again have the opportunity of meeting you
personally.

Sincerely,

Richard Nixon

His Excellency Yitzhak Rabin
Prime Minister
Jerusalem, ISRAEL

bcc: Rabbi Baruch Korff

LA CASA PACIFICA
SAN CLEMENTE, CALIFORNIA

December 17, 1975

My dear friend,

As the year 1975 comes to an end, I
want you to know how deeply I have
appreciated the loyal friendship and
support you have extended in such full
measure.

The most precious gift any person can
give to another is friendship, and for
the privilege of yours I shall always
be grateful.

Sincerely,

Richard Nixon

*Mrs. Nixon join
me in sending our
best wish for a
very happy New Year*

*Letter of appreciation from President Nixon to Rabbi Korff, Dec. 17,
1975.*

LA CASA PACIFICA
SAN CLEMENTE, CALIFORNIA

May 8, 1976

Dear Friend,

I have been enormously impressed by Walter
Annenberg's new publication "American Views"
and have ordered a year's subscription for
you.

I am sure you will find the objective coverage
of national and international issues refreshing
and encouraging by providing balance to the
overwhelming liberal bias which has infected
so many of the nation's leading columnists and
commentators.

Sincerely,

Rabbi Baruch Korff
351 Winthrop Street
Rehoboth, Massachusetts 02769

November 10, 1976

My dear friend,

As has been the case so many times in recent
years, my thoughts turn to you, filled with
deepest gratitude for the privilege of your
friendship and never-failing loyal support,
no difference how formidable the obstacles
nor heavy the seas.

Your commitment to and leadership of the
Justice Fund efforts which made it possible
to initiate and carry on the continuing
constitutional legal battles represent as
eloquent an example of the innate goodness
and compassion of man as has ever been
demonstrated. I shall forever be grateful
to you for the energy and dedication which
you have given in such full measure to this
project.

Mrs. Nixon and I join in sending our heartfelt
best wishes and warmest personal regards to
you and your family.

Sincerely,

Rabbi Baruch Korff
Rehoboth
Massachusetts   02769

*Letter from Nixon thanking Korff for his work in the Justice Fund,
Nov. 10, 1976.*

La Casa Pacifica

Dear Rabbi Korff,

You, Rebecca and
Zamira were ever so kind
to send me the generous
check as a birthday surprise.
It brought joy to the
day and happy thoughts
of your treasured friendship.
Having endorsed it for the
Justice Fund, I am enclosing
it in this note along with
a postal money order which
was received from another
friend.

All of our family send
deep gratitude for your
loyal support and your
prayers.

With all best wishes,
Devotedly,
Pat Nixon

Personal notes to Rabbi Korff from Pat Nixon.

La Casa Pacifica

Dear Rabbi Korff,

I was deeply disappointed to have missed your visit to San Clemente and now look forward to the "next time."

Rose Gaunt has told me of your kindness in wanting us to have a weekly bouquet of roses. What a thoughtful person you are to plan such a delightful surprise!

With constant appreciation for your many kindnesses over the years and with

warm best wishes to you and your family from all of us - your admiring friends!

Gratefully,
Pat Nixon

September 11, 1990

577 CHESTNUT RIDGE ROAD
WOODCLIFF LAKE, NEW JERSEY

Dear Rabbi Korff:

I want you to know how deeply Mrs. Nixon, Tricia, Julie, and I appreciated your very eloquent letter of July 19th. It was a very special day for all of us and your presence there would have made it even more so.

Under separate cover I am sending you a certificate of appreciation for the part you played in making it possible for a library to be constructed and a photo album containing pictures of the four Presidents, the four First Ladies, and other V.I.P.s who attended the ceremony.

With warm regards,

Sincerely,

Rabbi Baruch Korff

Final note from Nixon to Korff.

THE VICE PRESIDENT

WASHINGTON

STATEMENT BY VICE PRESIDENT GERALD R. FORD FOR RABBI KORFF

Section I of the 25th Amendment to the United States Constitution, the same part of the Constitution under which I was nominated and confirmed as Vice President last year, states:

"In case of the removal of the President from office or of his death or resignation, the Vice President shall become President."

On December 6, 1973, I stood before Chief Justice Berger, placed my hand on a Bible held by my wife, and swore a solemn oath to "support and defend the Constitution of the United States" and to "bear true faith and allegiance to the same, without any mental reservation or purpose of evasion."

Your question therefore asks me whether under hypothetical circumstances I would be willing to disobey the Constitution and violate that oath. My answer must be that I could not do so under any circumstances.

Statement by Vice President Gerald R. Ford for Rabbi Korff.

Korff might have adapted from Antony's speech, "his word might have stood against the world. Now he lives in California, and none so poor as do him reverence."

I can just see Korff holding the vast audience in the palms of his hands and then throwing the hooker: "If you have tears, prepare to shed them now."

Korff had no chance to deliver that speech of his.

During the convention, invitations to address small groups often came surreptitiously, but I managed to urge hundreds of delegates and alternates to care about the dethroned President. I encouraged the sympathetic among them to visit Casa Pacifica and to offer tangible support to the Justice Fund.

I spoke with Nixon half a dozen times by phone and knew what the omission of his name meant to him. One time he contacted the head of the Kansas City Fairness chapter, Carolyn Dunaway, to leave a message for me to call.

He particularly objected to the absence of his picture from the giant lineup of Republican Presidents on display in the arena. He suggested that I make prominent use of Mrs. Pendleton, whose home he had visited, and that I try to address the convention. He asked how many delegates I had urged to visit him. I gave him names as well as numbers. He mentioned something he wished I had said in the Brokaw interview, then added, "I know you can't think of everything."

Biographer Stephen Ambrose and author Robert Sam Anson say that Nixon's campaign advice to Ford included: "Don't worry about what you say about Nixon. Murder me. I understand." That must have come after the convention had made Ford the nominee.

Six months before, Nixon had demonstrated a similar ambivalence when he flew to China after promising Ford he would stay out of the public eye until the November election was over. His trip came four days before the primary in New Hampshire, where Ford was trailing Reagan in the polls. Its timing drew widespread condemnation. Bill Buckley called Nixon a "pariah." *Washington Post* columnist David Broder, who had praised the pardon, cited "the utter shamelessness of the man." Barry Goldwater hoped he would "stay over there." Even the conservative *Manchester Union Leader*, which supported Reagan, thought it was a "miserable way" for Nixon to repay the man who had pardoned him.

25   John Mitchell

I got to know John Mitchell, Nixon's first-term Attorney-General, at the Fairfax Hotel, his hangout while he waited out the appeal of his January 1975 conviction for the Watergate coverup. The Fairfax was owned by the Gore family. Mary Gore Dean, who helped manage the hotel, was Mitchell's companion. Her late husband, Gordon Dean, onetime chairman of the Atomic Energy Committee, had died in a plane crash.

At the time, John was estranged from Martha Mitchell. It was Martha's public statements about leaving him because of the "dirty things that go on" in politics that led John to resign as manager of Nixon's 1972 reelection campaign two weeks after the Watergate break-in. The reason he gave was concern about his family.

Mitchell kept pretty much to himself in a corner of the hotel dining room, and I joined him from time to time. As he struggled to come to grips with his fall from the heights of Cabinet official and ranking Wall Street law partner, his attitude was more disbelief than self-pity. "A man destroyed by his own explosive devices!" he would mutter.

But one time he said, "Men I treated like my own children conspired against me," referring to John Dean and campaign deputy Jeb Magruder, whose testimony implicated him. "They wrote their own scenario, interpreting every nod, downwards, upwards, sideways. I was their scapegoat."

Over coffee one day, I asked Mitchell, "Aren't you also on tape?"

"Nothing incriminating," he said. "I usually met with the President in his living quarters or talked to him on a secure line."

"Meaning what, exactly?"

"Nothing that you don't already know. My mistake was in men, not in law."

Indeed, he had told me before that he met with the President in the solarium and kitchen of the White House "many times" within a "10-day period" a few weeks before the Watergate break-in on June 17, 1972. "No one was present—no one was allowed," he said, adding, "I never did anything without his approval." I later learned that the family and even Manolo Sanchez, Nixon's valet, had been told to let the two fend for themselves.

Our exchange reminded me of something Nixon had once asked me in the den at San Clemente in late 1974: "Don't you think that everyone agrees now that I didn't know beforehand of the burglary?" That was the moment I realized that if he told the whole truth, he might never recover, privately or publicly.

One day I raised the subject of Agnew with Mitchell. Mary, who had joined us at the table, started in, "I'll tell you why they couldn't have sparred with Spiro—" John raised his eyebrows and Mary stopped in mid-sentence.

She completed the sentence the next day: "You should know that Spiro was Nixon's hatchet man, just as he was Eisenhower's, and you don't fire a hatchet man. John is by nature insular and reluctant to open old wounds."

Louise Gore, Mary's sister, was even less inhibited. She'd held various political positions in Maryland and was the Republican nominee for governor in 1974, losing handily to Marvin Mandel, who was later indicted.

"We like to wrap a halo around people in high office as if they were untouchable. I know where the bodies are buried," Louise said. "Spiro was not alone, and he climbed the ladder of success because he was on the take. His downfall was due to carelessness."

When it came to the game of who knew more about whom, Louise was without peer. "Let me tell you something about that paragon of virtue, Barry Goldwater," she once said. "I was a leading solicitor in his campaign for the presidency. I walked into his inner office one evening with cash and checks and found his desk cluttered with bundles of cash. And I mean cash with a capital C. When I offered to help him count it so he could store it, he said, 'No, it would take us all night. Just separate the checks and stuff the cash in bags.'"

I prevailed on Mary and John to attend a Citizens' Congress banquet at the Mayflower Hotel on December 13, 1975. They received a standing ovation from the more than a thousand diners.

Their table was a considerable distance from the dais, where Earl Butz and William Simon were seated. At some point Butz said to Simon, "Bill, let's go down and lift his spirits." Which they did, thereby winning a niche in my heart. A few days later, back at the Fairfax, Mitchell said simply, "Thanks. It felt good to be among friends."

I called Mitchell in the spring of 1977, the day before he started his nineteen-month prison term. "Is there anything I can do?" I asked.

"No, no," he said. "Your prayers, that's all."

"My call is not perfunctory," I tried to explain.

"I know, and I appreciate it more than I can say. You are a great friend, and I value your friendship, but there is nothing anyone can do." His voice trailed off with a rasp of distress.

He was alternately resigned and defiant. "They got what they wanted, but I am not down. I'll live through it. There's nothing I did that I wouldn't do again with a clear conscience."

"They that hate thee shall be clothed with shame," I said.

"My mistake was in men, not in law," he replied. Then we said goodby.

26   The Shah Betrayed

In August of 1977, Ardeshir Zahedi, the Iranian ambassador, invited Zamira and me to his embassy for lunch. Zamira, whom Zahedi seated at the head of the table and told, "You are the lady of the house," was bedeviled by the attention. My initial curiosity, however, grew into misgivings about the "assignment" the lunch led to.

Zahedi proposed that I visit the Shah. It was a time of growing unrest in Iran, with the mullahs led by Ayatollah Khomeini fanning resentment against the Westernization of Iran. The Carter Administration did not "fully comprehend the nature of the problem," Zahedi said. "The mullahs are against our alliance with America. It is insurrection." He cited the importance of Iran as a listening post on the Soviet Union and said, "Without the Shah, the U.S. will be banned in Iran."

Zahedi, the Shah's former brother-in-law, thought my connections with Congress might help him to lessen the disagreements between our governments. He had previously sponsored a planeful of high-profile visitors to Iran, including Elizabeth Taylor, Nixon aide Jack Brennan, and a score of politicians from both parties.

He mentioned several unpublicized dealings between Teheran and Jerusalem. Some of them I was already aware of—that Israelis were training Iran's military and intelligence units, as well as its border patrols on the Gulf, and that Iran had been supplying Israel with "a good deal of its oil." Later, I sent a written report of our exchange to the State Department via Senator Jacob Javits.

Zamira kept asking, "When are we going?" and at the end of our visit I tentatively acceded to Zahedi's request. "Incidentally," he asked, "who is your physician?" I told him as we were ushered into his limousine for the trip home. Asked what she had learned from the lunch, Zamira replied, "That you can eat asparagus with your fingers."

The next morning, my doctor, Gerald Foster of the Harvard Medical School, called to ask what was going on. Later that day a messenger from the Iranian embassy arrived with four first-class tickets on Iran Air. My attorney, Edward Cooperstein, used the fourth.

Zahedi's persistence made me wonder what we were getting into. His broad hints of possible enrichment for me and my causes had made me uncomfortable. I had not been to Iran before, but I had met the Shah at an international gathering in Egypt.

I cleared the trip with the State Department and asked friends in Israel how it might serve them. Their answer was "oil." I wanted to visit Egypt, Israel, and Jordan as well, so I called Zahedi to have the tickets adjusted. In the end, we bypassed Jordan because of an outbreak of cholera there. Zahedi also found room for a friend of Zamira's and the friend's mother.

Our flight to Iran, delayed until October because of my previous commitments, might as well have been by magic carpet. We had the whole first-class section of a Boeing 747 to ourselves. The crew's hospitality was as overpowering as the champagne and caviar they served. Two Iranian lieutenants, one male, one female, attended us from the moment we reached JFK Airport until we landed at Teheran.

There, we were encircled by a security contingent led by Hussein Emami, the Shah's chamberlain, and put into two limousines, bypassing immigration and customs. With sirens blaring and three security cars of palace guards, we whizzed to the Royal Hilton with such speed that it was difficult to make out any landmarks through the drawn curtains.

Zamira and I were given a three-bedroom suite with living room, kitchen, and study. Soon stewards and waiters appeared with rolling kitchens. I began to wonder about the price of it all. A U.S. embassy official appeared to say that Ambassador William Sullivan invited me to call. I still didn't know what was expected of me.

The next day Emami and his security detail escorted us to the palace. My meeting with the Shah lasted forty-five minutes and consisted largely of grievances against the Carter Administration. Its decisions, the Shah felt, might have been motivated more by a desire to repudiate Nixon than to set an independent course toward Iran. He gave me several documents supporting his views that I passed on to sympathetic members of Congress.

Implying benefits for me, Zahedi had said, "A tanker of crude oil will go a long way," and the Shah also mentioned a tanker of crude. I told them both the same thing: "Give it to Israel."

The Shah looked as if he were embalmed in wax, in marked contrast to the first time we met. He questioned the wisdom of his reliance on allies. He said that the mullahs were "ignorant people who settle with God at the expense of the people while we choose to settle with the people for the sake of God." Afterward, he graciously took the time to meet the others in my party.

Our stay in Iran lasted ten days, during which I visited Isfahan, Qum, and Persepolis, the opulent city the Shah had erected to honor his adopted ancestors. I talked with mullahs and pro-mullah merchants, meetings arranged by Emami, who had relatives among the opposition. On Zahedi's advice, the Shah wanted me to get an accurate assessment of that opposition to enlighten the Carter Administration. I was given one of the audiotapes that Khomeini had made in Paris to rally his supporters.

Zamira, Cooperstein, and Dr. Foster made the Persepolis trip, and Dr. Foster went to Isfahan as well, in addition to visiting medical facilities in Teheran. I also managed to secure an introduction to Iran's oil minister for Richard Aldrich, a businessman friend from Providence, and his colleague, João Anjos Rocha of Lisbon. They had arrived three days after we did.

I called on Ambassador Sullivan, whose optimism about the Shah's prospects I did not share, and later reported on the trip to officials of two countries. But the only certain beneficiaries of my journey were Israel, which got that tanker of crude, and the Harvard Medical School. The school had applied to the Shah for a donation, and, at Dr. Foster's suggestion, I put in a good word. The school ended up receiving $15 million.

In less than a year and a half, the mullahs would dispossess the Peacock Throne, which received no help from the United States, its long-time beneficiary. And the terminally ill Shah would be homeless, moving from Panama to Mexico to the United States—until our embassy in Teheran was taken over in retaliation—then to Egypt, where he died in 1980. All in all, a shameful episode in U.S. diplomatic history.

Ironically, the only one in our group whose head wasn't spinning at the royal treatment we received was Zamira. She had been meeting heads of state since she was six and considered it normal.

Shortly after the Iran trip, Nixon drove me around Casa Pacifica one day in his golf cart, pointing out the helipad, Coast Guard station, Secret Service command post, and the flower beds around the housing complex. We then went to the upstairs den where he had once spent several hours with Leonid Brezhnev. At the White House, he had explained how the sixfold increase in the exodus of Soviet Jews in 1972 had come about:

> Brezhnev wanted the U.S. embargo on technology to the Soviet Union lifted to gain access to our medical advances. Nixon felt Russians lose respect if you give them something for nothing, so he said, "What about showing some departure from totalitarianism, for which you're so widely criticized, and letting some refuseniks out? I'm prepared to offer any number of entry visas."
>
> Later, in a letter to Nixon, Brezhnev described as "indispensable" the information three Soviet medical experts obtained on a visit to the National Institutes of Health.

In the den at San Clemente, Nixon reminisced about Brezhnev: "He's smart but has the mind of a peasant, uncouth and slovenly. . . . Decisions of immense consequence to the world were made right here. . . . This is the chair he favored [a dark brown, overstuffed leather chair]. . . . I found him simple but cunning."

He would lapse into silence, then resume: "We confronted the Chinese head-on. . . . We faced up to the challenges of a troubled world." He yearned for what had been. His physical health was restored, but certain memories lingered. Mercifully, Manolo Sanchez appeared with drinks and hors d'oeuvres.

The caviar had a familiar taste. I'd just received some containers from the Shah, via Ambassador Zahedi, and told Nixon so. "How is his Majesty?" he asked, and I filled him in on my trip. Later, we joined Mrs. Nixon for a dinner of trout and other welcome dishes, each served with Manolo's assurance of its kosher content. It was a relaxing and revealing evening.

27 Mission Accomplished

Fairness had concentrated on the Midwest and South, where our recruitment potential was greater, and Kentucky was among the most fertile states. Many Kentuckians signed on with the Citizens' Congress and contributed to the Justice Fund.

In May 1978 Representative Tim Lee Carter of Kentucky and Elaine Hartman, a fiery operative in Washington's conservative hierarchy, urged me to participate with the former President in the dedication ceremonies for the Richard M. Nixon Recreation Center in Hyden, Kentucky, population 500.

Hyden, in a coal-mining county that was 80 percent Republican, was part of Kentucky's fifth congressional district, the nation's poorest in the 1970 census. Funds to build the $2.7-million center had come from the revenue-sharing program Nixon had initiated.

Given the traditionally inhospitable climate toward "outsiders" in Leslie County, I was delighted to accept. The timing—July 2nd—also coincided with my promotion of the *Richard Nixon Memoirs*, particularly 1,000 deluxe autographed editions.

In late June, however, a letter arrived signed by Leslie County Judge-Executive C. Allen Muncy. "This is so very, very special to the people of Leslie County," the judge wrote, "and space in the center is so limited that I cannot displace my local people with out-of-state guests." I got the message.

Although four years had passed and it was Nixon's first public speech since resigning, no Kentucky Republican leader attended the dedication. Nor did former President Ford, who had turned down an invitation before Nixon was asked, according to Robert Sam Anson in his book *Exile*.

No matter, it was the opening shot of Nixon's public comeback. In September he delivered a eulogy at the funeral of his friend Elmer Bobst in New York City and granted press interviews. In November he addressed the American Legion in Biloxi, Mississippi, following enthusiastic airport receptions en route at Dallas and Shreveport.

He told the Shreveport crowd, "Officially, you can say I'm out." The *New York Times* editorial writers did not care for that message and said so, but it was true. And my role faded. Bruce Herschensohn thought that was only natural. "You are the Day of Drums in the emerging years of triumph," he told me.

28   What Price the First Amendment

The elastic standards sometimes applied to the noble concept of a free press never ceases to amaze me. A notable example is the account by syndicated columnist Mary McGrory of the third annual Leadership Awards Dinner of the Citizens' Congress Education Foundation.

The dinner, on Washington's Birthday 1978, raised funds for a program the Foundation had inaugurated two years before to bring foreign students to Washington to witness the operations of the legislative branch. Six university students, two each from Egypt, Iran, and Saudi Arabia, were to begin internships on Capitol Hill that June.

The dinner's honorees were President Anwar Sadat of Egypt and Senator Russell Long of Louisiana. Also commended, for their roles in resolving Washington's 1977 Hanafi hostage crisis, were Ashraf Ghorbal, Ardeshir Zahedi, and Sahabzada Yaqub-khan, the ambassadors from Egypt, Iran, and Pakistan, respectively.

The guests included forty-seven members of Congress, sixty-one foreign diplomats—among them nearly half of Sadat's cabinet, led by Dr. Boutros Boutros-Ghali—thirty-two members of the intelligence community, eighty-three from the military, and leaders in the arts and sciences, industry and finance.

As at all USCC functions, the dinner's leadership drew from the Fairness Committee and its satellite organizations. Nixon's soon-to-be-published memoirs were specifically promoted from the dais. Perhaps that is why Miss McGrory—after noting the presence of liberal Senators Abraham Ribicoff and Jacob Javits and conservatives Anna Chenault and FDR associate Tommy Corcoran—chose to describe the event as "an evening with Rabbi Korff." She wrote:

> You might have thought that in 1974 when Richard Nixon left town, Rabbi Korff might have gone too, or at least gone underground. You would be wrong. He didn't even drop a stitch. He was all over the event like tear gas.

"The rabbi called on them in his commanding gutturals, 'Stand up, Admiral Turner. Where are you, Admiral?'" Miss McGrory wrote, adding that I "ordered the senators around like pages." She continued:

Then he briskly bade the senators and congressmen to come forward for the presentation of the "Pharaonic concept" which the Congress Foundation is bestowing on Sadat. It was a large statue of a young woman with an exceptionally big dove perched on her arm. The rabbi impatiently ordered the legislators to hoist the thing high. They strained like furniture movers.

And:

The rabbi does not look back. He is onto other things and, as usual, has had no trouble getting a foot in the door. He had a long, apparently earthy, chat with Sadat in Cairo on Dec. 29. He shared some of their confidences with the audience.

And finally:

The rabbi is [the Foundation's] shepherd, and it shall not want. The price of the tickets ranged from $2,500 for sponsors (who included Henry Ford and the Gulf Oil Corporation and, inevitably, Rabbi Korff) to $25 for people who just came to dinner. The take has not been counted, but the hall, a hearing room in the Dirksen Senate Office Building, was full.

My accent, of course, is what it is. It may be foreign, but my heart is domestic. Miss McGrory, however, seems to go well beyond the allowance we all have to make for the difficulty of seeing ourselves as others see us. Orrin Hatch of Utah, a first-term senator who attended the dinner, shook his head in disbelief at the column.

About the meeting with Sadat, whom I had first met in 1967, there is little to say. It was at Sadat's request, and he cited it in his periodical, *October Journal.* Doubtless he wanted an "unofficial" courier who had access. I passed on what he wished me to, to U.S. officials and to Moshe Dayan, who was to be involved in the Camp David negotiations the next year. Zamira found our meeting "boring," so Jihan Sadat "borrowed" her, showed her the Sadat family's menagerie of animals, and, with the President, signed her diary. "There was a big monkey and a giraffe," Zamira reported.

After the McGrory column appeared, Senator Claiborne Pell, in charge of Senate housekeeping, wrote to the Foundation's head, Senator Carl Curtis, advising that future events held on Senate premises would have to conform to the Senate's rules, which forbade fundraisers. As far as I have been able to discover, the Foundation was the first organization the rule was applied to, though not the first it could have been applied to.

It was something of a family disagreement. I had met Pell's father, Herbert Claiborne Pell, when he was the U.S. representative on the War Crimes Commission at the end of World War II. The Pells were one of New York City's earliest families, as Pell Street in lower Manhattan and several geographical Pelhams near the city's northern border attest. Indeed, Bertie Pell served briefly as congressman from Manhattan's Silk Stocking District.

As a lifelong Democrat in that Republican district and in Republican Newport, Rhode Island, the family's subsequent base of operations, he was used to doing his own thinking. He was the kind of man who told a funeral director that his late father would be no less distinguished a person laid out in a pine box as in a fancy casket. And who, to illustrate why business subsidies were uneconomic, wrote an article showing that a pineapple industry was possible in Norway if the subsidies were high enough.

Indeed, Bertie Pell resigned from the War Crimes Commission because he objected to the United States and the Soviet Union each averting its eyes from the other's German scientists to protect its own.

He was also the kind of man who moved from London's Cavendish Hotel to the Ritz because his son would be visiting. In the words of Admiral Strauss, who knew the Pell family well, he thought the cosmopolitan clientele of the Cavendish made it "rather too *louche* for a young man's residence."

Bertie Pell took me under his wing, upbraiding me if I was late and literally telling me how to tie my shoes. I felt about him the way I felt about another cherished mentor, Pope John XXIII, whom I worked with in rescuing Jews during the war, when he was papal nuncio in Turkey.

Pell senior introduced me to his son in London when the future senator was an ensign in the Coast Guard.

After I moved to Rhode Island, I raised funds for Senator Pell's reelection. In 1990, while visiting Providence, President Bush sent for me to ask me to support the senator's opponent, on whose behalf he was in the city to make a speech. I told him I simply couldn't.

For his part, Clay Pell is a trustee of the Baruch Korff Foundation and kept an eye on Zamira, who was on the staff of the Senate Foreign Relations Committee, which he chaired until 1995.

Another broadside fired at my defense of Nixon was a 17-page article entitled "Thinking the Unthinkable About the Nixon Scandal." It appeared in the December 1976 issue of *Atlantic Monthly.* The article's would-be "smoking gun" was the Justice Fund. Its author, Renata Adler, wrote:

> It stands to reason that, although there may be contributions every time the Rabbi calls a press conference (among the largest of them are those of the DeWitt Wallaces and, strangely enough, those of Rabbi Korff himself, who is paid a salary by the Committee from which he contributes to the Fund), citizens are not racing to send in their checks for the former President's legal defense.

Here are the facts. Yes, I contributed to the Justice Fund, but no, I never received a salary from the Fairness Committee or the Citizens' Congress. The money I live on comes mostly from family and friends who have looked out for me for years, augmented by stipends from the U.S. government for speechwriting and profiling, and a modest pension from Massachusetts for my work as a chaplain. Before August 9, 1974, my travel expenses on behalf of Richard Nixon were covered by Fairness. Afterward, they came out of the Citizens' Congress, including my efforts for the Justice Fund.

Yes, the Wallaces of *Reader's Digest* contributed generously, but not to the Justice Fund. Their donations went to the Fairness campaign, out of concern for the Republican Party, and to the Citizens' Congress, neither of which benefited Nixon financially. Indeed, DeWitt Wallace once told me, "I support your ideology, but I don't want Nixon to survive. He will injure the conservative cause."

Having warmed up, Miss Adler, who interviewed me at length, speeds down the runway and takes off: "If one accepts, for a moment, the proposition that the awful secret that underlay the Nixon Administration was money . . . there is a question what would have happened to the money and how the former President could reach it now."

Piling up conjectures about secret Swiss bank accounts, she tells of global intrigue with "German investors in I. G. Farben, which became the American company General Aniline—the depositors in those accounts were likely to be former Nazis who were precluded from access to their investments under American law."

Miss Adler speculates: "As for how Nixon could reach the money, however, there are several possibilities. There is, for instance, Rabbi Korff."

Wow! Is it any wonder the IRS audited me five times after Carter became President, resulting in one refund, three "no changes," and denial of one of some thirty charitable contributions? The disallowed $100 gift was to a yeshiva in Israel, which was not listed in the IRS book of approved exemptions.

Fortunately for me, my accountant, Joel Kane, does not charge for preparing my tax returns. Instead, he contributes to my causes and serves on the board of the Baruch Korff Foundation, which provides grants to authors and scholarships to students, and over which I have no control. Miss Adler continues:

> Whatever else is true, it is clear that Rabbi Korff has access to money and both the opportunity and the explanation for conveying it to the former President.
>
> Korff's background has always been international, not to say swashbuckling. In the early forties, he was, he says, raising money to buy passports in Paraguay for Jewish inmates of Nazi concentration camps and, by means of contacts in Switzerland, paying money to Himmler to get those prisoners out. There follows a period in which, Korff says, he spent a lot of time abroad, raising money for the Stern gang and the Irgun. When one asks raising money from whom, the Rabbi becomes vague and laughs.
>
> In the fifties and sixties, Korff actually had a congregation, a small one, and wrote a lot of speeches, he says, for Democratic congressmen. He now travels a lot abroad. And it proves, of course, nothing more than that the former President has got a loyal, well-traveled,

fund-raising friend, whose declared source of funds—
citizens sending in a dollar here, a dollar there—would
not amount to much or make much sense.

It has also been probable from the first that those
"loans" from Robert Abplanalp and Bebe Rebozo were
never loans in any normal sense. They were not meant
to be paid back. Nor were they gifts. What seems clear
if one pursues the records and this line of reasoning is
that the money Nixon's friends have "loaned" him is in
fact his own, which he cannot, for one reason or
another, reach any other way.

Miss Adler did get one thing right—about Nixon
having "a loyal, well-traveled, fund-raising friend." As
thin as the air is for the rest, let me try to respond:

• I sure wish I had known about all those secret
millions before I ran myself ragged for five years making something like a thousand fund-raising appearances, at least a hundred of them for the Justice Fund.

Less than 1 percent of the $358,000 raised by the
Fund came from foreign sources. Three major donations that I know of, from heads of state in response to
my appeals, went directly to Nixon without passing
through me or the Fund. Doubtless there were some
others like them.

Furthermore, I am much too disorganized to handle
funds effectively. I merely had contributions sent to our
office. The processing of all checks and monitoring of
balances were done by other officers of the organization.

I have heard of radio personalities inundating listeners with tales of astronomical caches awaiting the "Prisoner of San Clemente," though without Miss Adler's level of "detail." But I certainly would not have felt the need to make Pat Nixon's birthday check as sizable as it was if I had not seen the Nixons' straitened circumstances in a hundred ways first-hand—from the shabbiness of the Casa Pacifica grounds to Manolo Sanchez serving for some time without pay because he was unwilling to leave.

What I saw with my own eyes were the volunteers the ex-President had to depend on to handle his mail. What I heard with my own ears more than once was Nixon thanking me on the phone, then asking, "Can you make another payment?"

The total of his legal bills was actually far more than we raised. In his 1990 book *In the Arena*, Nixon put the figure at "over $1.8 million." The annual property taxes alone on Casa Pacifica exceeded $37,000. Even the cost of his life-saving surgery and hospital stay in October 1974—$23,000—had to come from his own pocket because he was not insured for it.

Gradually, Nixon worked his way out of his financial pit, with the Frost interviews, his memoirs, and the sale of the Key Biscayne and San Clemente properties. But in the beginning his estimated $80,000 annual pension from his White House and congressional years was not nearly enough. He needed the help he got from friends— with the Casa Pacifica mortgage, for example—and collateral relatives and the Justice Fund. The first two years after his resignation were touch-and-go.

• As for being vague about who supplied the funds I raised, I believe in honoring the anonymity of those who request it and in any case see no point in identifying benefactors of groups in pre-Israel Palestine when the subject is Nixon's finances. That said, major contributors to the Justice Fund included:

Frank Fitzsimmons of the Teamsters; Othal Brand of McAllen, Texas; Gabriele Pendleton; Ellen and Melvin Heller of New York City; Elizabeth Taylor; the Propps; Joseph E. Fernandes; Grace and Henry Salvatori; Mabel and Lloyd R. Johnson; Louise and Jack Kahn; Joseph Coors of Golden, Colorado; Helen Clay Frick of Pittsburgh; Jay Willard Marriott of Washington, D.C.; General Albert C. Wedemeyer of Boyds, Maryland.; Admiral Arleigh Burke of Bethesda, Maryland; Edwin and Miriam Soforenko of Providence, R.I.; and former Treasury Secretary William E. Simon.

These people and others I have identified as contributors many times before.

• I have had three congregations in my rabbinic career: Haym Solomon, one of the largest in New York City, 1938–40; Temple Israel, Portsmouth, New Hampshire, 1950–53; Agudath Achim, Taunton, Massachusetts, 1954–71. I continue to serve Agudath Achim in an emeritus, fill-in capacity.

While at Agudath Achim, which served twelve communities, I was also chaplain to the Massachusetts Department of Mental Health, ministering to more than a thousand patients and their families in and out of custodial care.

• My speechwriting over forty years was bipartisan, not just for Democrats, and was on behalf of the Senate, State Department, and White House. As it happens, I was a major fund-raiser for the 1966 campaign of Edward Brooke of Massachusetts, the first Republican senator to call for Nixon's resignation.

• All I know of Robert Abplanalp comes from hitching one ride in his executive jet back to New York City following a visit to Key Biscayne. He struck me as a calculating businessman. Bebe Rebozo I know to be as uncomplicated and virtuous as the desert wind.

That the vast majority of the print media in the United States called for Nixon's ouster does not diminish my appreciation for their traditional role in defending our liberties—even when I find them errant or overly adversarial. But I suspect that Miss McGrory's bile, Miss Adler's flight of fancy, and Miss Quinn's deception in 1974 would have made Jefferson and Thomas Paine blush.

29   The Legacy of
Watergate

Richard Nixon was a complicated man. I arrived at the Casa Pacifica gate one day in early 1975 with two Fairness people who wanted to meet him, Jean Baldwin and Diane Jacobs. We were turned away. The voice on the intercom said that Nixon didn't want to see anyone that day.

On my next visit, I asked about the turndown. Nixon threw his arms around me, said he had never been told, and blamed Ziegler. But Ziegler insisted that Nixon had been told and had said no.

Why circumvent the truth if a perfectly good excuse is available? Anyone who has recently had major surgery has bad days. One circumvents, I think, only if one feels that the real reason cannot safely be given.

In 1985, a Nixon assistant replied to an invitation

from the Episcopal Bishop of Rhode Island, George N. Hunt, for Nixon to become honorary chairman of the Rabbi Baruch Korff Endowed Scholarship at Brown University. "The former President has a policy," the assistant wrote, "of not accepting honorary chairmanships of charitable, academic, or other undertakings."

I was hardly unused to rejection. I once received the following message from a prominent Brahmin banker I had known for years: "I can never respect a man whose hero is a criminal." He wrote it across the face of an invitation to be a trustee of the Baruch Korff Archives at Brown, a collection focusing on the rescue of Jews during World War II, Israel's founding, and Watergate.

I had several letters like that. And Nixon did contribute to the scholarship and the archive fund. But to be rejected by both sides was a new experience.

The Republican officeholders who defended Nixon during Watergate did so largely on the basis of his private assurances to them that he had known nothing about the break-ins and had no role in the coverup. I cited a similar assurance in my appearances on his behalf. And when the June 23rd tape removed all doubt about his coverup role, those officials were left hanging. Many of them were defeated when they ran for reelection.

In the political fraternity it is considered a "mortal sin," says Saul Pett of the Associated Press, "to let the other fellow catch your mud in his eye without at least a whispered warning to duck." Hence Chuck Wiggins, on being shown the June 23rd transcript by Haig and

Nixon attorney James St. Clair, saying bitterly: "The guys who stuck by the President were really led down the garden path, weren't we?"

Nixon consolidated his enemies, not his friends, because he did not understand, or could not bring himself to meet, the obligations of friendship. Such as loyalty being a two-way street. The migrant nature of the California he grew up in—the absence of roots established for generations—was probably a formative element in that uncertainty, affecting both his own values and the values his early constituents expected of him.

He was the most self-conscious of men, as if he had no idea what standards to measure himself by in personal relations and therefore adjusted his performance for each individual. More than anyone I have ever known, he was a chameleon. I constantly had to revise my reading of him. It was more than having my heart go out to him on one visit and being taken aback the next. It was that the conclusions I drew were regularly contradicted.

Biographer Stephen Ambrose notes that many long-time Nixon associates were shocked at the tape transcripts because they portrayed a Nixon they had never seen. I was not really surprised, however. Perhaps the dual nature of our meetings—political support and pastoral—exposed me to a greater range of the Nixon persona than outsiders usually see.

Surprisingly for a career politician, Nixon did not meet people easily. His preference for crowd applause was as much for the distance between him and the crowd as for the approval. He would close a love letter with "sincerely yours."

The lack of the standards of self-measurement traditionally considered to comprise "character" tends to erase the distinction between objective merit and public relations. Hence the imperviousness toward criticism that allowed him to rebound again and again throughout his career, prompting critics to say he was without shame. That is why I believe that admitting everything after resigning would have inhibited his recovery as well as his reemergence.

The same deficiency in standards, however, assured that enemies far outnumbered friends when he most needed friends. Perhaps because he was given more to self-pity than trust, Nixon's career centered on negating, not affirming, which in the long run also limited the pool of potential friends.

Kissinger was understandably angry that his talks with Nixon had been taped. Even conversations with friends were recorded. In Nixon's two offices and the Lincoln Sitting Room, the taping system was voice-activated and operated automatically when he was present. Only in the Cabinet Room was the system manual.

But why not let people know they were being taped? That simple courtesy would not have been likely to change what they said except possibly to make their statements more thoughtful. I felt that the President's ethical obligation to those who did not know was sufficient grounds for destroying the tapes, quite apart from what was said on them (an opinion Nixon apparently came to share by 1980, in a TV interview with Barbara Walters—seven years too late).

On Fairness's first visit to the White House in December 1973, I told Nixon what I thought and asked him, "Why didn't you make a bonfire on the South Lawn and burn the [expletive deleted] tapes?"

"Where were you when I needed you?" he quipped, then added, "After it became public, even before they were subpoenaed, it might have been considered tampering with possible evidence."

The logic offered by his 1978 memoirs on the point is even more compelling:

I was also persuaded by Haig's reasoning that destruction of the tapes would create an indelible impression of guilt, and I simply did not believe that the revelation of anything I had actually done would be as bad as that impression. . . . I made a note outlining this rationale: "If I had discussed illegal action, I would not have taped. If I had discussed illegal action and had taped, I would have destroyed the tapes once the investigation began."

Finally I decided that the tapes were my best insurance against the unforeseeable future. I was prepared to believe that others, even people close to me, would turn against me just as Dean had done, and in that case the tapes would give me at least some protection.

But that logic works only when premised on innocence. When guilt is the premise and the tapes are the only irrefutable evidence, it is a dangerous charade.

Haig's advice assumed innocence, as did the advice of everyone except perhaps Mitchell, Haldeman, and Colson. But somewhere beneath his denial mechanism, Nixon knew better. His posture of innocence required him to keep the tapes, he felt, but he never would have had to resign without them. Sophocles worked with less plot than that.

By all historical standards, Nixon belonged in the Oval Office. Few Presidents had his grasp of global relationships—of using strength to give peace efforts a chance to endure—and the skill to navigate the crosscurrents of international and domestic politics in pursuit of his goals. He demonstrated these capabilities in the Middle East, in the U.S. disengagement from Vietnam, in the détente with the Soviet Union, and, from a career basher of Communist China, in the opening to a quarter of the world's population.

Elliot Richardson, the Attorney-General who resigned rather than obey Nixon's order to fire Watergate prosecutor Archibald Cox, made the point well. "To a degree greater than any other [postwar] president," Richardson said in 1983, Nixon had a "strategic sense toward the opportunities of office."

History will not permit carping at Nixon's motives to demean his accomplishments, and neither should we today. I have no doubt, for example, that his help for Soviet Jews was motivated by the coming 1972 election and that 150 Soviet Jewish families were admitted to the United States in early 1974 in hopes that the impeachment lobby might ease off. Indeed, he more than doubled his Jewish support in 1972 over 1968—from an estimated 16 percent to 37 percent—and received 75 percent of the Hasidic vote in 1972.

Watergate might even have been a factor in Nixon's rearming Israel during the Yom Kippur War, though balance in the Middle East and between the superpowers was the overriding purpose. But none of this carping matters, because responsiveness to the concerns of the electorate is at the heart of the democratic system. Richard Nixon earned my people's pardon.

I am confident that his domestic initiatives, too, will meet history's test—energy independence, revenue-sharing, student loans, welfare reform, government reorganization, national health insurance—even if some of them were more initiative than accomplishment because of Watergate.

In the words of the Quaker poet for whom the town he grew up in was named, I believe that "the safe appeal of Truth to Time" will acquit Nixon well. With some of his critics, however, I am less certain of acquittal. Theirs is the lasting downside of the Watergate legacy.

The revolution in communications technology that has brought congressional hearings into the living room strains fair play for incumbents—and fair-trial rights—to the breaking point. That press accounts of such hearings are no longer the filter through which voters learn what is going on perhaps constitutes progress. But the wonderland of live national coverage and instant polling is instilling the Red Queen's credo of "sentence first, verdict afterwards."

Absent strict procedural safeguards for hearings in such a wonderland, where is the perspective needed for informed opinion? Where on earth can an impartial venue be found? The United States' role in the world is far too important to be undermined by such shallowness.

Then there's press behavior. In Kennebunkport, Maine, in August of 1992, President Bush and Prime Minister Rabin together revealed a plan for peace in the Middle East. The historic moment was punctured, however, by the following question: "Mr. President, what do you say to the report in today's *New York Post* that you had an affair with your aide in 1984?"

The infection of the mainstream media by supermarket-tabloid standards may have more to do with an audience raised on television and its lowest-common-denominator pursuit of maximum ratings. When Armageddon rhetoric and 30-second treatment of news stories are the norm, the casualty is the shades of gray by which merit is determined. But it was during

Watergate that the White House press corps adopted supermarket-tabloid standards.

The nation's understanding of a President's performance is hardly helped by a sanctimonious media. For one thing, saints usually make weak leaders, particularly in foreign affairs, as Jimmy Carter showed. For another, such as the posturing of Sam Ervin's Senate Watergate Committee, all I can say is, God save us from the saints who haven't been caught.

30   Looking Back

Twenty years after Watergate, I see some things a bit differently. I am less inclined to condemn the way Republican leaders handled the problem Watergate posed for their party. And I respect the viewpoint of Nixon critics with no political axe to grind, such as my old friend Marvin Rubinstein of New York City.

I used to defend Nixon to Dr. Rubinstein by citing the frequent need for United States operations abroad to be conducted in ways that could not meet constitutional standards and the duplicity of the ideal diplomat: "When he says yes, he means maybe. When he says maybe, he means no. When he says no, he's no diplomat."

Dr. Rubinstein would point out that while the constitutional writ might not run to behavior abroad, subverting domestic elections was subverting the basic dispute-resolution process prescribed by the Constitution.

"Nixon did not have a mandate to lie repeatedly to the American people on American soil to cover up domestic crimes," he would say. "We are, after all, a government of the people, by the people, and for the people. You can't just be duplicitous with the people who elected you."

Still, I am proud of having defended Nixon and would do so again. True, my assumption of his personal innocence was rendered "inoperative" by the June 23rd tape. And yes, the vilification I received for my efforts did wound. Even today, I sometimes wonder whether I was the only non-conspirator among Nixon's intimates who suffered from that association without benefit of personal gain.

But I don't think any of this matters nearly so much as the dangerous precedent of allowing the presidency to be weakened by forces motivated essentially by politics. History should be the judge, and it properly evaluates Presidents by the effects of their official policies. Had the legal ramifications of Watergate been prolonged for another eighteen months, Nixon never would have had to resign and Watergate would barely rate a footnote.

The justification for defending Nixon is all the stronger given the singular talents he brought to the presidential office and what we now know that other Presidents did. Here is biographer Stephen Ambrose on the latter point:

The cover-up was not unique, nor was the payment of hush money, nor the attempt to use the FBI and the CIA and the Justice Department to obstruct justice. There was ample precedent for most of these actions, as there was for the break-in at Dr. Fielding's office, the placing of wiretaps on reporters and NSC officials, the surveillance techniques, or the dirty tricks in the 1972 campaign; there were ample precedents for the ITT scandal, the milk fund, the bombing of Cambodia, the attempted use of the IRS to get his enemies, and Nixon's personal enrichment through improvements on his homes in California and Florida. . . . Two wrongs do not make a right, not even in politics, but they do make a precedent.

I also admit to an occasional wistfulness about the Fairness plans that never got off the drawing board. One was to bring a million protesters to the nation's capital. I can recall our transportation committee planning the acquisition of 10,000 buses, some from Canada, to accommodate people who lived within 600 miles of Washington. Those from farther away would be flown in.

A march on foot from Los Angeles was also considered, our numbers swelling en route. One option discussed was to have the protesters ring the capital and paralyze government. Another plan was to engage all the members of the House Judiciary Committee in their districts for the 1974 election, and half of the more vulnerable senators as well.

We estimated that such plans would cost on the order of $25 million, which we could not raise. I discussed these plans with Donald Kendall. I thought that he or White House aide Peter Flanigan might have the connections for that kind of funding. But events did not work out that way.

In 1975 Bebe Rebozo said to me, "If it hadn't been for you, Richard Nixon would have been destroyed and forgotten." His gracious overstatement aside, I am immensely gratified by Nixon's eventual role as elder statesman. No righteous man is without sin, the Talmud says; no sinner is beyond redemption. Nor can any nation afford to ignore a source of wise counsel.

I have always tried to put to the best use I could the years my mother bequeathed to me as I huddled against her, lying in the streets of Novograd-Volinski in 1919, moments before she expired from a pogrom's bullet. An inner voice shouting, "Coward! Coward!" soon cut through my five-year-old fears, and my life ever since has been a quest for redemption from that charge.

"A man either lives forever," my father used to tell me, "or not at all." Through various causes, including the defense of Richard Nixon, I have tried to be guided by that admonition as well. I like to think that both my parents would have approved of something Bruce Herschensohn once wrote: "Rabbi Korff is a small-town rabbi the same way Sam Ervin is a country lawyer."

Epilogue

A Letter to the Grandchildren of Richard Nixon

If I were your grandfather, I would say to you that my goal has always been to leave behind a worthy legacy that would endure beyond time. During my years as the thirty-seventh President of the United States, I strived to set precedent for lasting judgment and erred when I followed precedent that fell short of that mark.

I could speak volumes of my rendezvous with destiny, always in sight of the Divine—of my union with your grandmother, the only woman I have ever known; of your mothers, Tricia and Julie, two pillars of unbounded valor; of your fathers, Ed and David, who stood with me in days of drums; of my odyssey in my eighty-one-year pilgrimage; of trial and error, denial and fulfillment. But there is already an ocean of published words.

In your wisdom you will ferret out the good from the bad, the benign from the malignant—of this I have no doubt. So too do I trust the objective historian to portray my presidency as indigenous to the soil that is America.

I look to you as the repository of my hopes; the interpreters of my dreams; the heirs of my heritage, which is steeped in the Pilgrim fugitives from injustice and refugees from persecution who carved their resolve in granite like the faces of my predecessors on Mount Rushmore.

I made the leap from what might be considered by today's standards a log cabin to the house hallowed by a pioneering nation, for the pioneers of yesterday built America and the pioneers of today preserve America. The indomitable spirit reincarnates itself in every generation.

Your grandmother and I hovered about your mothers as your mothers and fathers now hover about you. And when shadows dance in my twilight, I raise my lantern to your glowing eyes and beaming faces and pray that they will never fade from memory. The rhythm of your pulses, the rhapsody of your laughter, the gaiety of your feet, your harp and song reverberate in my being as I close my eyes and settle into nostalgia.

From the depths of my soul, the core of life that binds me to you, I profess my love unabashedly. I am bound with you no less than with my country, whose soul I kept in trust for you and for all Americans who share its plains and rivers, its mountains and valleys, and give meaning to life and labor, to hope and prayer. In the words of Kahlil Gibran, "When you love, you should not say, 'God is in my heart,' but rather, 'I am in the heart of God.'"

The President and I

Appendix

Phil Shabecoff of the *New York Times* described my interview with the President as providing "an unusual self-assessment of a public figure who has closely guarded his personal privacy throughout his career."

During our two-hour interview, the President's eyes glistened and his voice turned hoarse when he spoke of the attacks on his family; he was tense and halted to clear his throat. He was solemn on the subject of world peace and morose at being sidetracked. His mood alternated between sadness and serenity, joy and sorrow, and a mixture of supplication and regret, with an occasional sigh and a quiver in his voice. He appeared self-conscious and apprehensive when the subject was Watergate.

He tended to leap around, so his chronology was difficult to follow and had to be edited. I have also deleted some parts for "reasons of taste and legality," as had been suggested.

INTERVIEW WITH THE PRESIDENT
at the White House, May 13, 1974

THE PRESIDENT: Well, let me say that I am very grateful for your support. We are going through some pretty hard times, and this is when we test the strong people. The people have to believe very deeply to fight like you do.

RABBI KORFF: Well, it stems from faith. We were reared on faith and, therefore, it is no problem here. King David once asked his jeweler to fashion him a ring, which is simple for a jeweler, but King David also asked him to inscribe something, a passage on the ring that would be applicable in times of joy and in times of sorrow. And the jeweler couldn't find a passage that would fit both joy and sorrow until he came upon Solomon, who was twelve years old at the time, and Solomon asked the jeweler, "Why are you so downcast?" And he told him of his problem, and Solomon said, "Why it is simple. I have just the passage for you: `This too shall pass.'"

When you look at it in time of joy, you will not be overjoyous, you will be so with moderation. And in time of adversity, you will know that this, too, shall pass. And so, what I really feel, Mr. President, is that this is entirely in your hands.

Some time ago I wired you and presumptuously asked you not to yield one jot or tittle, and my conviction is this: that you have everything to gain and nothing to lose. Just the other day, in talking with one member of Congress who was relatively quiet, and he said to me, "Well, I had to come out with something because the media ignored me when I expressed favorable comment. So, as much as I am up for re-election in November, I had to."

But in the final analysis, Mr. President, I think that this is the time to insulate yourself, totally and completely. You are constitutionally right. In a question-and-answer period talking about the tapes, I said there are two elements I can see there. When Mr. Dean first entered, the President immediately said the thing must come out. The facts must be made known, and it was only after Mr. Dean said that "I am involved and others are involved" that the President assumed a paternal attitude.

It was easy to cast him to the wolves, easy, and then, too, if you notice as you go along in the transcript, there is that devil's advocate to get at the truth, which was fed to you slowly, slowly and bitterly, the height of a man's disappointment, and so on. If you were not a strong President, but a weak President, you would immediately cast him to the wolves, but because you are a strong President, you examined all the options.

And then I pointed to my own counseling area. A couple came to me with their son, a junior at the university, who was indicted by the U.S. Attorney for using drugs and selling drugs, and I sat for two hours with this couple examining every option. And you would think that I was subverting the law, how I might influence the U.S. Attorney, how to appeal, who do we know we can call to influence him, how we can approach it.

In my heart, Mr. President, you have grown tall like the cedars of Lebanon.

Now I have a number of questions, Mr. President.

THE PRESIDENT: You go right ahead.

Q: We are preparing a paperback. Now, you might be interested in this. This is a subdivision of our committee, which is Task Force I [passing material to the President].

A: You really hit it right on the nose.

Q: We try to do that. Now, in addition to it, we are calling for a Citizens' Congress on June 9th, and I would like very much, Mr. President, if you could have both the letter which goes out to our delegates and also the schedule.

A: You want me to keep this?

Q: Yes. A friend of yours, a Mr. de Toledano, who has known you, he said, for twenty-five years, says he has never once heard the President make a racial slur. When he was Vice President, Mr. Nixon chaired a President's Committee on Government Contracts, which quietly broke down discriminatory barriers.

In 1950, when the President was accused of antisemitism, the Anti-Defamation League backed him totally. Now, I know, Mr. President—and as Senator Goldwater is fond of saying, "In your heart, you know that I am right"—I know, Mr. President, from my brief association—and I researched my soul—that there is not an ounce of prejudice in you.

But I, nevertheless, would like very much to have your comments on this.

A: Well, as far as the charges that were made, they have perhaps even by this time been totally denied by Mr. Buzhardt yesterday and Mr. Garment today, but be that as it may, the critical point is what the attitude of whoever is President is toward all races and all religions. Now, I would say in terms of antisemitism, first, you have to be judged by your actions. There has been no stronger supporter of Israel than myself. Mrs. Meir will tell you that. Without the airlift and without the alert, Israel would probably not have survived.

Q: And even then, you stood alone.

A: I overruled a lot of people within the Administration. Now, the other point is, of course, this: that if there was any attitude which would suggest antisemitism, why would I have appointed Walter Annenberg ambassador to London?

Let me tell you, many of the so-called Eastern elite objected to his appointment. They didn't say it was because he was Jewish, but deep down that was the reason some of them objected. I can assure you, too, that the appointment of Henry Kissinger as Secretary of State was strongly opposed, despite his brilliance, and in this instance, many thought, because of the delicate negotiations that had to take place in the Mideast and the fact that we depended some on the Arab countries for our oil.

But to be quite truthful, we must recognize that in every country, including America, there is an "anti" strain. Some people are antisemitic, some people are anti-Catholic, some people are anti-black, some people are maybe anti-Italian or -Polish or what have you. But when we look at this Administration, the Secretary of State, the Chairman of the Council of Economic Advisors, the Chairman of the Federal Reserve Board, the Ambassador, the highest ambassadorial post in terms of distinction that can be granted—all are held by men of the Jewish faith.

So, ask them. The point is the actions give [the] lie to the fabricated words.

Q: Thou shalt be known by thy deeds, and this is precisely what the transcripts reveal.

A: Yes. As a matter of fact, I will tell you an interesting thing on that score, too. When I appointed Mr. Schlesinger Secretary of Defense, a high-ranking official, whose name I will not mention because it would not be—I wouldn't even want an implication against him, and he no longer serves in a position where he can influence policy—but a high-ranking official who was very interested in the Arab-Israeli conflict said, "Do you know Schlesinger's background? Is he Jewish?" And I said, "I haven't the slightest idea. I have never asked him."

And he said, "Well, he has a Jewish name." I said, "Well, I don't know what that proves." I said, "The reason I picked Schlesinger is that he is the best-qualified man to be Secretary of Defense," which, of course, is the same reason that I picked Kissinger—because he was best-qualified to be Secretary of State.

And incidentally, one of the reasons that I have strongly opposed the quota system is that a quota system discriminates against those who may be the ablest among our very diverse population simply because they may not be the most numerous.

Q: At this point, Mr. President, I would like to go to a number of questions, if I may, and I would like to cut my questions to a minimum so as to enable you to elaborate.

Sir, among the questions I would like to raise is one that deals with a fact that amazes even your worst political critics. How do you stand up under the kind of vilification and attack and savagery that has gone on for the past year and a half? What enables you to persevere?

A: Part of it is inheritance—strong mother, strong father, both of whom worked hard and were, incidentally, deeply religious. And second—and I don't put these necessarily in the order of priority—a very strong family, my wife and my two daughters and my two sons-in-law, all of whom stand like a rock against attacks when they are made.

Third, good support here on the White House staff. You need strong men like General Haig and in the Cabinet as well, and there are many in the Congress, friends generally around the country, like yourself.

But in more personal terms, it gets down to what the Quakers call peace at the center. And my peace at the center, which my mother, who was a Quaker—my father was a Methodist, and of course when they married, they both became Quakers—but in any event, peace at the center means that whatever the storms are that may be roaring up and down, that the individual must have and retain that peace within him, and that will see him through all the adversity.

I think the other point which I think is enormously important for any individual who knows that he must go through some pretty tough times is, frankly, just having been through the battle. Throughout my life I have not had it easy. I worked hard as a boy. I worked my way through school.

Oh, the Navy was not all that difficult, but in politics—

Q: You volunteered, of course.

A: Oh, yes. Everybody was volunteering in World War II. Nobody should get any brownie points for that.

But the point is that in my whole political career, I have always been usually at the very center of controversy. I would be fighting for and talking for what I believed was right. And consequently, I attracted opposition, as any individual does who stands up for unpopular positions, what may be unpopular, but which may later turn out to be right and popular.

Any individual, under those circumstances, develops an attitude which builds an immunity. Not a thick skin; I don't like that term. That connotes insensitivity, because even with peace at the center, an individual has great sensitivity.

I would not suggest that unwarranted attacks—and some are warranted, I mean no one is perfect—but attacks, particularly when they are against family and friends, as well as the individual, they hurt you.

But the individual cannot succumb to the attack, or take the easy way out, like resigning the office, as I could have on other occasions by not running for the office in the first instance, taking the easy way out after a defeat, or thinking, "Well, I will go out and make money," which is very easy for me, being a fairly accomplished lawyer.

Q: Fifty percent of your net assets you made as a private attorney practicing law.

A: And now they are gone. But in any event, I feel that the very fact that I have gone through defeat, defeat for the presidency, defeat for the governorship, and then had to fight hard throughout my political life for many causes that were at times unpopular, including the very, very difficult period of the war in Vietnam, which was here when I came and which is not here now.

Many of my closest friends right within the Administration would have preferred that I dump that responsibility on my predecessors and bug out. I could not do that, because I knew that if the United States did not stand firm where a small country was concerned, that South Vietnam and no other small country in the world would be safe again, that none of our allies would have confidence in us again.

I do not mean to suggest that I see war as something that we must always defend or as a diplomatic tool which we should be quick to use, because again, because of my background, at the heart I have a very strong revulsion toward armed force, any kind.

I remember my mother and my grandmother both cried when I went into World War II, very quietly, because as Quakers, they understood that I had to make my own decision, but I went.

The main point, however, is—and I have digressed a bit here—but the main point is that as I saw the whole terrible struggle in Vietnam with thousands upon thousands demonstrating around the country and marching around the White House, I saw it as being one of those times that this country had to pass through and that we had to come through in a way that we did not dishearten our allies or the neutrals or give encouragement to those who might embark on aggression.

And that is why I insisted on ending it in what I think is the right way.

Q: As some of your friends have said, that had you not settled the Vietnam War in Southeast Asia and brought back our prisoners of war, the movement, this unsavory alliance against you, would never have taken place. They would still be marching and raising the Viet Cong flag for peace in Vietnam.

A: Yes, well, in fairness, though, there are many who did not oppose my policies—which did end the war in the right and responsible and honorable way—who still favor resignation for other reasons, so I give them credit for that.

But what I am suggesting is this: Your original question was how does an individual stand it. How do you stand the savagery, we will call it viciousness, sometimes libelous, so forth, of critics, etc., etc., etc.? I have expressed several things:

One, in order to go through a great crisis, you have got to have been through some, and I have been through plenty.

Second, it must be inheritance, training as a youngster. I inherited something from my father and my mother, both of whom are very strong, shall we say, frontier-type people.

Third, the support of good friends who stand with you when it is tough.

And fourth, it gets down to something that can't be described in words, and that is, some would call it a sense of fatalism. But it isn't exactly that, because one must make his own fate. He must not simply toss on the sea and not attempt to swim to land. There is a way to go to land.

There is a sense of what I have described that I have had through all the tough periods, most of all the tough periods, whether in defeat or in victory, and that is that I don't change at the center. I don't go overboard when we win and I don't get terribly depressed when we lose. I don't go overboard when things are good; I don't go overboard when they are bad. And it is keeping an even keel.

The Midwesterners had a term. They say, "Stay steady in the buggy." Well, we don't have buggies anymore, so how we would translate that to present-day idiom, I wouldn't know. But the most important factor is that the individual must know, inside, deep inside, that he is right. He must believe that. If, for example, these charges on the Watergate and the coverup, etc., were true, nobody would have to ask me to resign.

I wouldn't serve for one minute if they were true. But I know they are not true, and therefore, I will stay here, do the job that I was elected to do as well as I can, and trust to the American constitutional process to make the final verdict.

Q: How would you rate the performance of the White House press corps?

A: I know, for example, in the press room that my policies are generally disapproved of, and there are some, putting it in the vernacular, who hate my guts with a passion. But I don't hate them, none of them. Individually, I understand. Their philosophies are different, they don't agree with my positions, and after all, they want to write and take me on. An individual must not return hatred for hatred, and I am saying this not in moralistic terms. I don't believe in wearing morals on my sleeves.

Someone has referred to the fact that I wasn't constantly moralizing with my staff on these tapes. I think it is the height of hypocrisy to sit and lecture an adult about his morality.

But my point is what really destroys an individual when he is under attack is if he allows the hate against him to become part of himself, and then the fury that arises within him will destroy him.

I suppose if you were to take it out of the New Testament, you would say, love your enemies. Politically, we have to know that in this system there has got to be room for different points of view, and if an individual in this office ever allows himself to be blinded by his hatred of those who hate him, then he won't do a good job; he won't do the right job.

The only way I have been able to continue to go forward on the initiatives at home and abroad as I have during this past year—whether it is in the Mideast or in negotiating with the Soviet Union, continuing the dialogue with China, or whether at home, pushing for our health program and our education program, as I did today in a meeting with Cap Weinberger, pushing for programs that we trust will bring inflation under control—the only way I am able to do those things is not to be consumed by what consumes my friends in the press room.

So I think you could put it this way: They are consumed by this issue, and I can see—not all—but I can see in the eyes of them not only their hatred but their frustration. And as a matter of fact, I really feel sorry for them in a way, because they should feel strongly and they should write strongly, but they should recognize that to the extent that they allow their own hatreds to consume them, they will lose the rationality which is the mark of a civilized man.

Q: Mr. President, I would like very much for you to record, can you tell us how you think historians fifty years from now will assess Watergate, how they will assess that in relation to other events and the achievements of your years as President?

A: Well, I can first indicate a hope, and perhaps my prediction will be, shall we say, the result of a hope. As I read history, what really matters as far as leaders are concerned is what they did on those great issues that affect the great masses of the people, for good or for bad.

I do not mean to say that political abuses should be overlooked, whether conducted by our side or conducted by the other side.

I never went to a meeting without having not only a demonstration, but in many instances violence. I don't blame Senator McGovern for it, because just as in the case of Watergate, sometimes overzealous people do things they shouldn't do, and some of the people who supported him acted violently, in many instances, as we know.

As people look back to the years of the seventies, Watergate will be written about as being something very difficult to understand, particularly coming in the campaign of an individual who is supposed to be a political pro, which I am. But as often said, I was so busy in the year of '72—and this is not said in justification, it is only said by way of truth—I was so busy with my overriding concern to get the war brought to an end, to do the right things on the domestic side, that had to be done, that I frankly didn't pay any attention to the campaign.

In years past, I have been criticized because I always ran my own campaigns, and sometimes I lost, perhaps because I didn't have anybody else running it for me adequately. In 1972, I don't mean to throw off on those who ran the campaign. They meant well, but I can assure you that had I been spending the amount of time on the day-to-day operations of this campaign and getting the reports, etc., that I always insisted on in my previous campaigns, Watergate never would have happened.

John Mitchell put it pretty well. They asked him, "Did you tell the President?" He said, "No." They said, "Why not?" He said, "Well, because I thought he would blow his stack." Well, he was right, I would have.

Now how will historians fifty years from now looking back on the United States of America and its role in the last third of this century, how are they going to assess Watergate? The point is, how did Watergate affect the election of '72? And the answer is, Watergate affected the election in 1972 only [by] reducing the margin that we won by.

Because it was a negative issue for us. Nothing was obtained there, as we knew. No information. It was not only wrong, but the wrong was compounded by its being totally senseless and stupid.

Q: Some people maintain that two of the burglars were on the payroll of the CIA at the time and five of the seven involved were in leading positions in the Bay of Pigs invasion when President Kennedy withheld air cover.

A: Well, I can say on that without attempting to put the cloak of national security over Watergate—which should not be done, because Watergate was a political operation—that unfortunately, among those who participated in the Watergate activity were people, some of whom had held very high positions in the CIA and others of whom had been in the Bay of Pigs. There is no question about it.

But getting back to how you appraise this Administration, the Administration will be appraised, I think, in terms, without being too melodramatic, in terms of how first we have made a major contribution, not only to peace for the United States, but a contribution of peace to the whole world.

I am praying right now that we can make progress in the Mideast and I am getting reports every day. If that should come, what a great thing that would be. Sometimes my friends of Israel say to me, "Well, we don't like the fact that you are being friendly with the Egyptians." Far better to have the United States a friend of Israel's neighbors than to have only somebody else a friend of Israel's neighbors.

Q: At this juncture, I might point out that Yitzhak Rabin, who is a friend of yours, has just formed a cabinet. He and President Anwar Sadat expressed identical sentiments, and they both said that Americans should not engage in this luxury of political rivalry, and they said to look upon your great contributions to peace in Southeast Asia and the Middle East and the world. Do you feel that will be the appraisal of the historians?

A: They will appraise, first, the fact that the war in Vietnam was brought to an end and in a responsible way. If people don't want to use the word "honor," that is all right with me. By "responsible," I mean in a way that maintains respect for the United States commitments to small nations all over the world, including nations like Israel, and our friends in Europe and others.

Second, this Administration will be remembered for the opening to China. Clare Boothe Luce said when they write history a thousand years from now, maybe there will be one line about President Nixon—he went to China. Why was that important? It was important not in terms of the eight years that I will be in this office, but it is indispensable in terms of looking down the road fifteen, twenty, twenty-five years from now, because one-fourth of the world's people live there.

They are among the ablest of the world's people. They will be a major superpower, and for the United States not to have a dialogue and eventually some sort of relationship in which we peacefully discuss our differences would be a tragedy of the greatest proportions.

And in my view the opening to China had to be made now. It had to be made while I was here, because it is right now that the U.S. has the power and the respect, and when China needs the friendship of the U.S. And later, when she no longer needs it, it would be too late.

The opening to Russia: I know that is controversial, but the alternative is for these two superpowers to continue to go on a mad race of building up their nuclear power, and eventually rubbing together some-place, a spark will fly and the whole world will be destroyed.

And then finally, on the domestic front, we have changed America in many effective ways, I believe. They do not seem important now, but we will have a health program which will guarantee for everybody the health insurance he needs.

Q: Isn't it the first time that the HEW budget exceeds that of the Defense Department?

A: As a matter of fact, we have changed the priorities completely. When I came into office, the part for Defense was approximately 45 percent and the part for domestic was 35, and now it has turned around com-pletely.

We no longer have the draft for the first time in twenty-five years. But beyond that, domestically, we have changed government in the sense of turning power back to the people. Revenue-sharing means money goes back to the people. Our education program is based on the principle that local school boards rather than Wash-ington bureaucrats should determine how money should be used.

We will have made progress in cleaning up the environment. We will have made progress in a new transit system. We will have rebuilt our merchant marine. We have started to rebuild it.

And in addition, in the field of welfare, we have finally—it is gradual, but it is coming along—we have finally turned away from the welfare ethic to the work ethic. That means we have begun to establish the fundamental principle that individuals who can work should work.

And if you can't, you should go on welfare. So I would have to say this as a conservative—the kind of conservatism in the style of Theodore Roosevelt—that we look upon conservatism as relying on people rather than government, on individuals rather than government enterprises, to move America forward. Where the government plays an activist role, but where the government does not smother the individual, where the government does not make individuals so dependent upon government that the individuals become weak. Because when the people of this country become weak, America will become weak, and a weak America cannot lead the world.

The most important single factor—and I would close with this at this point on this issue—at this critical time in history, with every European nation and Japan capable of exercising prime leadership in the free world, the hopes for peace and freedom rest in this room. And as long as I am here, I am going to see that the office is not weakened.

And I want to pass on to my successor not only the office unweakened, but also a philosophy that America shall continue to lead for the balance of this century. Because if we do not, in the free world, there are others in other parts of the world who are willing to fill that vacuum. And this must not happen.

And this is not said in an anti-Communist or anti-Russian or anti-Chinese sense. As far as I am concerned, I like the Russian people; I like the Chinese people. I don't like their systems; they don't like ours. But I believe strongly that America, with all of its power, will never use its power to destroy freedom. Therefore, we are the great force in the world not only for peace—which we will not break, because we don't want war or conquest—but freedom, which we cherish. That is what we fought our wars about during this century.

And for that reason, therefore, getting back to impeachment/resignation, I can assure you that if a President becomes unpopular because he is being attacked about something where he knows he has not done anything wrong, for a President to then walk out of this office, the day of the strong American Presidency would be gone. Because Presidents from then on would be looking at the polls every morning to see whether or not they ought to do this or do that.

They would be wondering whether or not the Congress, if they didn't like this policy or that policy, might put in a resolution for impeachment. Or whether or not their colleagues in the Congress, of their own party, who were concerned about the election, might ask them to resign so that somebody else could take over and they would have a better chance.

It is essential that we have a strong Congress, a strong court, but above all a strong presidency in this period, because a strong American President, be he Republican or Democrat, is indispensable if we are going to be able to play—well, I would call it, play God's greatest role for any nation or any individual—the role of peace-maker in the world, for the whole world.

Q: Throughout the transcripts, Mr. President, there is a repeatedly stated concern on your part for the impact of Watergate on the lives of both those young men not involved and those caught up in this affair. Do you think an injustice has been done? Has there been a wholesale smear of the President's men in the Watergate affair?

A: Well, I would have to say that with the number of committees, with some of the activity—not of Mr. Jaworski, whom I respect very much, but of some of his eager-beaver staffers—that there has been an abuse of process.

If these activities, the kind of tactics that have been used—the harassment of secretaries and stenographers and people who can't afford lawyers, and so forth, hours and hours of drilling and questioning and threat-ening and all the rest—if these tactics had been used in the day of Joe McCarthy, he would have been ridden out of town on a rail.

I believe that when it is all sorted out in the end, it will be found that there has been harassment on a massive basis of innocent people, that many without guilt have had their reputations badly damaged. And I fear, too, that it will be found that many who have been charged with guilt have been charged on flimsy indictments, as was indicated in the Mitchell-Stans trial.

Q: And this is precisely, Mr. President—the *New York Times* ran almost an anatomy of a jury in which they couldn't believe that a verdict of acquittal or innocence is possible, and they took the jury to task in various ways. And in so doing, they have sought to instill in subsequent juries the fear of pronouncing innocence because this, in a way, proved [the] *Times* wrong. They had found Mitchell-Stans guilty long before.

A: Well, it is time that we recognize in this country that our system is based on the principle of trial by jury and not trial by the press.

I think much of the press has been responsible. I think much of the press—and particularly, I am sorry to say, much of the television press—has not been responsible. And I have seen men as a result of congressional hearings, as a result of inspired leaks and as a result of source stories, etc.—men who were not guilty—be badly damaged in terms of their reputations.

And I have seen them so tried, I have seen them tried and convicted in the press and on television, so that the chance for them to get a fair trial any place is almost impossible.

I would say it would be extremely difficult for anyone to get a fair trial, for example, in the District of Columbia now. That is no reflection on the judicial system here. There are many fine judges and fine people, but they have been exposed to the Seale rule. For example, in New York they have been exposed to such a barrage that it is very difficult for a jury to stand up to all that, even though they are sequestered during the course of the trial.

And I think that if one good thing could come out of Watergate—and some good comes out of every adversity—it would be a greater sense of responsibility on the part of the press, on the part of investigators and the rest, for the rights of individuals. Every individual, whatever he is charged with, whatever his crime, has a right to a fair trial, to be properly represented, and to be protected against the character assassination which occurs so often in the press and on television before he ever gets to trial and which, therefore, makes a fair trial impossible.

Q: And this is what Louis Nizer said this weekend in the Sunday edition of the *Washington Star* in "Opinion." He took to task Senator Ervin for creating a climate of guilt. He took to task Judge Sirica very strongly, and Louis Nizer is a liberal. And he said in this climate we are doing an injustice to justice.

A: Well, as you know, Rabbi Korff, I would not, under any circumstances, criticize Judge Sirica or any judge.

I will only say, though, that if I were a defendant's lawyer, I would have to argue very strongly that the individuals who have been hauled publicly before committees—and who also, in addition, have been slandered on television night after night through source stories and the rest—have had their chance for a fair trial destroyed.

Q: Mr. President, what is your—and I don't want to overstay—

A: Go ahead. That is all right.

Q: What is your overall assessment of the press and media coverage of Watergate? You just more or less answered it, but I would like it from beginning to end, briefly.

A: Well, let me say, first, I understand the interest of the press here in Washington, and the media, on Watergate. It is a fascinating story. I would only suggest that an historical assessment would be that it was, probably—to use the word "scandal"—the broadest but thinnest scandal in American history. Because what was it about?

It is an interesting thing about the young people you refer to. It is an interesting thing about John Mitchell, about Bob Haldeman and John Ehrlichman and Chuck Colson and Maurice Stans, all of these men, all of them served in this Administration with great dedication. All of them came here at great personal financial sacrifice. None of them received anything.

Now, of course, I do not mean that crime can only be measured in terms of whether or not you were paid something. But when they say this is like Teapot Dome, that is comparing apples to oranges and, shall we say, rather poor oranges, too.

I would suggest, in terms of Watergate, it has caught the imagination of the press for another reason—and I do not say this with any bitterness at all—but I am not the press's favorite pinup boy. If it hadn't been Watergate, there would probably have been something else. So now they have this. But I will survive it, and I just hope they will survive it with, shall we say, as much serenity as I have.

Q: Well, Mr. President, I am witness to this.

Do you believe, Mr. President, as some of your aides have stated, that your critics in the press, in politics, and in the pulpit are using [a] double standard to judge the errors and successes of this Administration against that of other Administrations? And by this I mean, to take 33 hours of tape or transcript, compared to 5,000 hours of labor for peace and tranquility, for livelihood for this nation, for progress. What are your views, Mr. President?

A: There is a hypothetical double standard, let's face it. I guess maybe we all have somewhat of a double standard where our friends are concerned. But I would say certainly as far as the nation's media is concerned, there has been a double standard with regard to this Administration's accomplishments and with regard to the coverage of this very, very difficult Watergate period.

A senator or a congressman will say something that is favorable and it seldom gets reported. As your friend that you talked to on the Hill told you, the only way he could make the papers was to criticize the President.

Q: That is precisely it.

A: And in a way, however, in defense of my friends in the press—and I have some—as they say to me, criticism is news. Being against something is news. Being for something is not news. And they are in the business of news.

But the point is that if I were basically a liberal by their standards, if I had bugged out of Vietnam, which they wanted, Watergate would have been a blip. They wouldn't have cared. But it is because I have not gone down the line with them that they care.

For example, my critics don't like my appointments to the Supreme Court. Why not? Only because they happen to believe in a conservative point of view—not a far-right, but a conservative point of view—with regard to the Constitution. And I had to fight to get four, and I had to lose two in the process.

But my point is that it is because basically this Administration has not pandered—and I want to be very precise here. Individually, I don't believe that any President has been more fair to the press—and I will tell you why. I know President Johnson and other Presidents who have been in this office used to regularly pick up that telephone and call an editor and raise the devil about a story about him.

I have been in public life twenty-seven years and I have never complained about a story and I have never hauled a reporter on the carpet. Oh, in press conferences, right, we give and take.

Members of the press ought to look deep within their own consciences to see whether they do have a double standard or whether they do not, and basically whether they would apply these same standards to a liberal who went along with them.

Let me put it this way—I digressed a moment ago. I try to treat the press fairly, and on an individual basis there is no animosity whatever. And I think most of them will say that to you. I have no animosity; I never show any personally. But second, I refuse to pander to their views.

And I don't ask them to pander to mine, but I do believe that they should treat anybody who is President, be he conservative or liberal, with exactly the same standard. I mean, I don't mind having my tax returns gone over with a fine-tooth comb, and I will pay the extra money. I have never cared much about money. If I did, I would have a lot of it, because I was out of office for eight years and still only entered here with a net worth of less than $600,000.

Q: To make a point, Mr. President, not to reflect unfavorably on your predecessor, that he retired thirty times a millionaire and was always in the government, and you will retire in 1977 and you will still have less than $1 million in assets.

A: I don't reflect on my predecessor.

Q: And this is something that concerns us, too, that none of your predecessors are alive to take up your battle. This has troubled us very much.

A: Well, when I leave this office, I will defend whoever is President. Not his views, necessarily, but certainly the office.

Q: Sir, do you believe that the motivation of those who seek your impeachment is ideological or political or personal malice? How much of it do you believe is genuine concern over the wrongdoing that took place in Watergate and how much is ideological?

A: It depends on the group. I would say that generally speaking, as far as the people in the media are concerned, it is an ideological thing. As I said, if I were a liberal, Watergate would be a blip.

As far as those in Congress are concerned, there are mixed emotions. Some are partisan, although many Democrats support me strongly, and some Republicans, I think, are concerned about the outcome of their own elections this November and feel that if the President were to resign, that their chances would be that much better. And that I understand. And so, in Congress you have some of it that is partisan, although not as much as you would think.

I think when a congressman or senator gets right down to the tough call, he is going to think a long time before he wants to impeach a President, unless he finds wrongdoing, which justifies impeachment. It is interesting to note the analysis that has been made of these transcripts, which were very difficult for me to put out.

But now the great majority of those who analyze them say they don't find an impeachable offense, but they don't like their tone. Well, I can say that if they were to tape the conversations of Presidents that I have known, they wouldn't like their tone either.

I mean, there has to be at times very pragmatic talk in this office, and I would say also on that score, I don't have any apologies with regard to having tried to give, say, Mr. Haldeman, Mr. Ehrlichman, the benefit of the doubt during a terribly difficult two-week period from the 15th of April to the 30th of April, when they left.

After all, they had served well. They protested their innocence. They still do. And I felt that I had to—as my conversations with Mr. Petersen and all the questions I asked him demonstrated—I felt that I had to be reasonably sure. If there was guilt, out they would go, but I had to be reasonably sure there was enough evidence that their usefulness would be destroyed and that they would have to fight from the outside.

And that, of course, was the decision. And it was like asking me to cut off one arm and then another to have these two men leave. And it was a terribly difficult experience, and I would have to plead—

Q: Compassion?

A: Well, I would defend with compassion, but I would have to plead to those who charged that I did not act as swiftly as I should, I would have to say yes. I will admit in that respect that maybe I should have acted more swiftly. But if one of them had been in this spot getting one story from one person, another story from another person, not knowing where the truth was—and we don't even know what the truth is today—then I wonder how they would have acted.

I believe that under our system it is terribly important that we not overlook, above everything else, the right of an individual to be considered innocent until proven guilty. But beyond that, when he is under attack, not to run away from him right away. That is the political thing to do.

But to stand by him, unless he either is guilty or admits it or unless he becomes, because of the charges, in some cases—and that was the case with Bob Haldeman and John Ehrlichman because they both still protest their innocence and I trust will be found innocent, along with the others—unless their usefulness is impaired.

But I guess compassion in a President is not considered to be a virtue anymore, particularly when it does involve men who were close to him in developing policies that were basically conservative policies.

Q: Mr. President, I will close with just two brief questions. You know I am very fond of Julie.

A: Yes, she is fond of you.

Q: And I was terribly pained when Mr. Robert Pierpont of CBS posed a question to her, saying, "Now this is not a monarchy. In our system, we do not visit the sins of the father—and so to speak, paraphrasing the biblical—upon the children, so why are you defending your father?" It was cruel, inhumane, totally, and Julie really somehow—and I am still thinking about it and I inwardly feel tormented that this is possible in our day and age and no one raised an objection.

And she came up very nicely. I believe she mentioned that fifty-five calls came in to her mother's secretary, "How did the family feel?" you know, and of course—

A: Well, let me say, I think we will all be judged by history, and if you were to check with Mr. Pierpont's colleagues, that most of them would not have approved of that approach. I would say that most of the men in the press, as strong as some of them are on this whole impeachment issue, most of them are ladies and gentlemen and would not have shown such bad manners.

Q: And finally, Mr. President, what would be the criterion which you believe that Congress should use to judge you in the impeachment vote if it ever gets to Congress? Our feeling is that the House Judiciary, many of them—you may not agree with this—are so indebted to the archdeacon of impeachment, Mr. Meany, due to his lavish support of them, but my feeling and the feeling of others is that it will be drawn almost on partisan lines.

A: Well, of course, it would be presumptuous for me to indicate what the Judiciary Committee will do. I have read reports in the press to the effect that it is probably likely that the Judiciary Committee would refer the issue to the House.

And then when the issue comes to the House, the members of the House have to bite the bullet. They cannot pass the buck. The idea that a member of the House will say, "Well, I can't judge this, let's send it over to the Senate," that is not our system. Each member of the House is going to have to study the evidence, search his conscience, and vote what he believes is right. And I think that is what he will do, and that is all I would ask.

Now, what criteria will he use? Well, a member of the House cannot, and I am sure would not, use the criterion first of the popularity of the President. We would have impeached over half of our Presidents in their second terms if that were a criterion.

The second point is that I don't believe that the members of the House, when they really think about it, will impeach simply because of their concern about the effect on their party, so to speak. I noticed recently that some of my good party members took umbrage at a statement that I made that it was not the party that mattered, it was the country that mattered.

Well, now, I am a party man. I am one of the few party men that has campaigned all over the country in good years and bad years, for weak candidates and strong candidates. I was one of the few who campaigned the country for Senator Goldwater in '64—and in '58, when there were no Cabinet officers except one, I was the only one out campaigning for our Republicans.

In 1954 it was the same story. In 1966 I was practically alone because most of these fellows were considered to be losers, but I never considered it that way. But, nevertheless, that should demonstrate my party credentials.

I am very much concerned about what happens to the party. I want the members of my party, where they are good candidates, to win in November. But however, if there are good Democrats—and I know many good Democrats—I will be for them.

Q: Regardless of party.

A: The country must always come before party, and at the present time a resignation or impeachment of the President of the United States would, in my view, have devastating consequences in terms of our foreign policy, would jeopardize the best hope we have to build a structure of peace in the world—the best hope we have had in this century or perhaps in two centuries. And also would have a very detrimental effect on our political system for years to come due to the fact that it would weaken the Presidency.

It would mean that every President in the future, as he sits in this office, would be afraid to make unpopular decisions, and most of the great decisions that have been made in our history have been unpopular and have been made by strong men. The moment that a President is looking over his shoulder down to Capitol Hill before he makes a decision, he then will be a weak President and he will always come down on the side of what appears to be the popular move rather than being a strong President coming down on the side of what is right for this country.

For that reason, among many others, I must fight the impeachment, and I must, of course, as everybody knows, refuse to resign. While it would be comfortable to sit on the sands of San Clemente and have all of this behind me, I owe an obligation to continue the work that I have begun in the field of foreign affairs and in the movement toward a peaceful world.

And second, on the domestic front, to continue to work for those basic philosophical principles of returning government to the people rather than having it centered here in Washington.

And third, and this is probably the major concern that I have in this whole impeachment/resignation talk and why the decision has to be one to fight it through to the finish and fight it through to win. And that is that if I do not fight, if I were to run away or walk off the job, and if I did not fight the impeachment as it comes before the House in some form or other, I would leave to my successor, be he Democrat or Republican—not just the next one but for all time to come—a precedent of a man mortally weakened from this process of destroying a President who was not guilty of a high crime or misdemeanor. If that were to succeed, this office will never have the strong President that is needed here.

And so, you ask what is the test that a man in the Congress should apply. In this case, you go to the Constitution. The Constitution is very clear. It is treason, bribery, or other high crimes and misdemeanors. And I have every confidence that these hearings—as long and as difficult and tortuous and misinterpreted as they will be—in the end will demonstrate clearly that the present occupant of this office is not guilty of any of those crimes.

Q: As you know, Mr. President, we have millions of Americans who believe as we do. We have pledged our resources and I would say in this battle, our lives actually, to see this through, knowing full well that you will emerge the strongest President in the twentieth century. And I know this because after this—

A: Well, we have our low points, and we have a few coming, but we will survive it.

Q: Don't worry about it. And I, I would like you to give this to Julie. I promised Linda. This is evidence that I fulfilled my—these are some of the materials that we send out.

A: Oh listen, I know what you do. Everybody tells us. You are our greatest advocate.

Q: Thank you, Mr. President, and I do hope if it is at all possible, should I have a couple of questions or so to complete my paperback, I hope you will find it—

A: Well, if we can't do it, if you could even send them in to me, I could dictate an answer, you see, into the dictaphone for you. How would that be, if there are just a couple of things you would like?

Q: Thank you very much.

Bibliography

Ambrose, Stephen E. *Nixon: Ruin and Recovery, 1973–1990.* New York: Simon & Schuster, 1991.

Anson, Robert Sam. *Exile: The Unquiet Oblivion of Richard M. Nixon.* New York: Simon & Schuster, 1984.

Barone, Michael; Ujifusa, Grant; and Matthews, Douglas. *The Almanac of American Politics, 1978.* New York: Dutton, 1977.

Bernstein, Carl, and Woodward, Bob. *All The President's Men.* New York: Simon & Schuster, 1974.

Drew, Elizabeth. *Washington Journal: The Events of 1973–1974.* New York: Random House, 1975.

Frost, David. *I Gave Them a Sword: Behind the Scenes of the Nixon Interviews.* New York: Ballantine Books, 1978.

Isaacs, Stephen D. *Jews and American Politics.* Garden City, N.Y.: Doubleday, 1974.

Korff, Baruch. *The Personal Nixon: Staying on the Summit.* Washington, D.C.: Fairness Publishers, 1974.

Lukas, J. Anthony. *Nightmare: The Underside of the Nixon Years.* New York: Bantam Books, 1977.

Meir, Golda. *My Life.* New York: Putnam, 1975.

Nixon, Richard M. *In the Arena: A Memoir of Victory, Defeat and Renewal.* New York: Simon & Schuster, 1990.

————. *The Memoirs of Richard Nixon.* New York: Grosset & Dunlap, 1978.

Powers, Thomas. *The Man Who Kept the Secrets: Richard Helms and the CIA.* New York: Pocket Books, 1979.

Safire, William L. *Before The Fall: An Inside View of the Pre-Watergate White House.* New York: Tower Publications, 1975.

Watergate: Chronology of a Crisis. Washington, D.C.: Congressional Quarterly, 1975.

Selected Notes

4   increase in exodus of Soviet Jews: Ambrose, 171

10–11   AFL-CIO data: *National Observer*, Feb. 2, 1974; *Nation*, April 20, 1974

11–12   Fairness operations: *Boston Herald Advertiser*, May 19, 1974; *Nation* , April 20, 1974

20   Talmadge comment: *Christian Science Monitor*, Sept. 17, 1973

24   15 groups visit White House: *New York Times*, May 19, 1974

34   Nixon's income taxes: *U.S. News & World Report*, April 22, 1974

44   Helms testimony: *Watergate: Chronology*, 66, 86, 238–39, 243, 262, 434

     Helms firing: Powers, 310–12

44–45   Butterfield questioned: *Watergate: Chronology*, 117-A

     Buzhardt role: Ambrose, 186, 193

     Woods on Butterfield: Anson, 102

45–46   White House transcripts: *Watergate: Chronology*, 610; Lukas, 663–67

46   Mitchell-Stans acquittal: *Watergate: Chronology*, 616

49–51   Thimmesch column: *Los Angeles Times*, June 13, 1974

52–57   July 18–22 Fairness convention: *Bedford* (Mass.) *Patriot* and *Toms River* (N.J.) *Reporter*, July 24, 1974; *Westford* (Mass.) *Eagle*, Aug. 1, 1974; *Washington Post*, Aug. 4, 1974
        McGrory column: *Washington Star-News*, July 19, 1974
        Supreme Court ruling: Ambrose, 394

56   Haynes Johnson interview: *Washington Post*, Sept. 19, 1976

59   Nixon interview: Korff, 41–70

59–60   Jewish reaction to tape: *Corpus Christi Caller*, Aug. 7, 1974

66, 68, Nixon on author's visit, summons Woods, hears
        phones, 75 ringing, urged not to resign: Nixon, *Memoirs*, 1067–69

73   special bank of EOB phones: *Ann Arbor News*, Aug. 8, 1974
        White House switchboard overloaded: Drew, 408

79–80   Ford on pardon: *Watergate: Chronology*, 789–791, 807–8

83   Nixon's only court appearance: Ambrose, 536

91   Ziegler firing urged: Anson, 93

100   Pat Nixon's stroke: Ambrose, 498–99

101–2   Nixon's TV and book deals: Anson, 101, 114; Frost, 6, 12

102   Haldeman blames Nixon, then co-author: Anson, 204–6

103   Witcover interview: *Washington Post*, June 6, 1975

106–9   Golda Meir excerpts on Yom Kippur War: Meir, 430–31, 440

110–11 Nixon Library: Ambrose, 576–78

113–14 Royko column: *Chicago Daily News*, Aug. 16, 1976

115–17 Frank column: *Wilmington* (Del.) *Morning News*, Aug. 19, 1976

117–18 Nixon advice to Ford: Ambrose, 501; Anson, 149
        Nixon trip to China: Ambrose, 489–91

119   Martha Mitchell's statements: Bernstein-Woodward, 92

121   Louise Gore, Marvin Mandel: Barone-Ujifusa-Matthews, 353, 358

130   Hyden, Ky., demographics: Barone-Ujifusa-Matthews, 322–23

131   GOP reaction in Hyden: Ambrose, 517–18; Anson, 191–92, 194

131–32 Nixon comeback: Ambrose, 519–20

132–34 McGrory column: *Chicago Tribune*, March 1, 1978

137–40 Adler article: *Atlantic Monthly*, December 1976

141   Nixon's expenses: Ambrose, 475

145   politicians' "mortal sin": *Austin American-Statesman*, April 6, 1975
        Wiggins' bitterness: Lukas, 744

146   Nixon associates shocked by tapes: Ambrose, 586

148   Nixon on preserving tapes: Nixon, *Memoirs*, 902

149   Richardson view: Royster column, *Wall Street Journal*, Oct. 5, 1983

150   Nixon's percentage of Jewish vote, 1968–72:
        15%–nearly 40%, *Time*, Aug. 21, 1972, Nov. 15, 1976;

17%–35%, Isaacs, 184–99

Hasidic vote in 1972: Safire, 570

155 precedents for Watergate: Ambrose, 592

Acknowledgments

I wish to express my appreciation to Tim Noble, a freelance editor in New York City, who strived to clarify the manuscript's language and chronology and assure its factual accuracy. On occasion he took issue with my penchant for platform rhetoric: "You're not rallying the faithful, dammit. You're writing history for a critical audience." For history's sake, I relented.

I would be remiss were I not also to acknowledge the library staff of Brown University and its curator of manuscripts, Dr. Mark N. Brown, who made available research material from the Rabbi Baruch Korff Archives.

Several political associates and opponents reviewed the manuscript for accuracy. Any errors that remain, of course, are my own.

Baruch Korff

About the Author

Born in the Ukraine in 1914, Baruch Korff represents the seventy-second generation of rabbis in his family, a line that includes Israel Baal Shem Tov, the founder of modern Hasidism in the eighteenth century, and Rashi, the commentator par excellence on Bible and Talmud whose writings influenced Christian thought, in the eleventh century. This, according to Professor Yitzhak Alfasi of Bar Ilan University, a leading genealogist of hasidic dynasties. Following a pogrom in 1919, during which he saw his mother killed, the author moved to Kozec, Poland. He came to the United States in 1926 for his bar mitzvah under the instruction of his father, who had been smuggled out of Russia in 1919 under a sentence of treason, then returned to Poland for his education. There he met Vladimir Jabotinsky and became an adherent of Revisionist Zionism.

The author was educated at Yeshiva Ohr Torah in Kozec (Korets), Yeshiva Torath Chaim in Warsaw, and Yeshiva Rabbi Isaac Elchanan (Yeshiva College) in New York City, where he was associate editor of *Hedenu,* a student publication, in 1933. He was ordained at Yeshiva Ohr Torah in 1934, and the following year he earned the advanced degree of Yadin-Yadin, in Talmud and law, at Yeshiva Beth Mordechai in Jerusalem.

Over the next four decades, his activities included:

1936–37: headmaster of Yeshiva Torath Emeth, Brooklyn, New York. 1938–40: rabbi of Congregation Haym Solomon, New York City. 1941–49: adviser to the Vaad Hahatzala, the Union of Orthodox Rabbis of the United States and Canada; adviser to the U.S. War Refugee Board; director of the Emergency Committee to Save the Jewish People of Europe; executive vice-president and United Nations observer of the Political Action Committee for Palestine. 1950–53: rabbi of Temple Israel, Portsmouth, New Hampshire. 1954–71: rabbi of Congregation Agudath Achim, Taunton, Massachusetts, then rabbi emeritus. 1954–74: chaplain with the Massachusetts Department of Mental Health.

In 1973 he founded the National Citizens Committee for Fairness to the Presidency and embarked on his personal relationship with Richard Nixon. In 1974 he founded the President Nixon Justice Fund and the United States Citizens' Congress.

In 1983 he donated his farm in Rehoboth, Massachusetts, to Brown University and moved to Providence to act as consultant to the university in conjunction with

Brown's acquisition of the Rabbi Baruch Korff Archives of more than 50,000 documents and memorabilia covering the author's career.

For the last fifteen years he has been a regular panelist on "Confluence," a Sunday morning discussion program on WLNE television, the CBS affiliate in Providence. Other panelists on the 30-minute program are George N. Hunt, Episcopal bishop of Rhode Island, and Father Peter Graziano, pastor of St. Mary's Roman Catholic Church in Mansfield, Massachusetts. The moderator is Truman Taylor.

Since the mid-1950s, the author has traveled extensively in the Middle East under various auspices. His other published writings are *Novograd-Volinski* (1933), *The Warrior's Manual* (1943), *Flight from Fear* (1953), and *The Personal Nixon* (1974). Twice married, he has two daughters by his first wife and one by his second.

The Child is Father
of the Man

William Wordsworth expressed an undeniable human truth when he wrote that "the Child is father of the Man." Rare, however, is the man who recognizes the import of that thought even as he lives it. Baruch Korff is such a man.

To a superficial observer, Korff's life would seem to be many lives. Countless Americans remember him as President Richard Nixon's confidant and most vocal supporter throughout the Watergate crisis, as the architect of the National Citizens' Committee for Fairness to the Presidency. The rabbi's faithful, here and abroad, undoubtedly remember him as their personal and spiritual benefactor, the man who saw them through the challenges and trials of their lives, and who constantly spurred them to thought with his pointed and eloquent admonitions. Men and women privy to the realm of international diplomacy know Rabbi Korff as a respected negotiator with countless missions to the Middle East and trouble spots worldwide to his credit, an expert who is still consulted by government officials for his skills. Historians of the post–World War II period know Korff for the role he played as liaison for Lehi (the Stern Group) and the Irgun Tzvai Leumi and as the Executive Vice President and United Nations Observer for the Political Action Committee for Palestine, all of which, in the 1940s, put him at the very forefront of the battle for the creation of the Jewish state. And historians of the war years are well aware—as are countless others who either lived through that terrible time or have studied it—of his prodigious efforts as Director of Rescue Activities for the Emergency Committee to Save the Jewish People of Europe and as a key advisor to the U.S. War Refugee Board and to the Vaad Hahatzalah of the Union of Orthodox Rabbis of the United States and Canada. In those roles, Rabbi Korff helped buy precious time and save Jewish lives by means that were condemned at the time by less passionate observers as outlandish and foolhardy—if effective. He assailed the Jewish *shtadlanim*, which assured his ostracism. "I am uncomfortable with the comfortable," he once remarked. "A loner, a maverick," the others retorted. "He doesn't belong. " How could he?

Those are the lives comprising the life of Baruch Korff the man. Their unifying principles are uncompromised concern for others, a deep commitment to helping fellow Jews, and, above all, a refusal to countenance the commonplace deterrents that prevent human beings from truly acting on their consciences. And their genesis, Rabbi Korff himself has observed, lies in Baruch Korff the child.

The first chapter of Korff's 1953 diary *Flight From Fear*, which was penned in a French jail where he was being held on suspicion of "terrorist activities" on behalf of Jewish refugees, describes the formative experience of his life, an event that transpired in 1919, when he was but a boy living in a Ukrainian town called Novograd-Volinski.

The town was, in a way, two towns, a Jewish one and a Christian one. The Jews had their three synagogues, and the Christians, their four Russian Orthodox churches; their sonorous bells are the resonant backdrop to the horrific paternity of Baruch Korff.

The rabbi recalls how the church bells, at times, actually unified the schizophrenic town. For, apart from summoning Christians to prayer on Sunday, they served, as well, as the town fire alarm during the remainder of the week. More often, though, their pealing just abraded the Jewish souls of Novograd-Volinski, a clangorous reminder of the deep resentment that lay not very deep beneath the surface of the society around them, an invasive commemoration of centuries of all too unchristian attitudes toward Jews.

And then the rabbi recounts the events of the autumn day that birthed the man he grew to be.

It was not Sunday, yet the bells tolled, and in each of the town's four churches; they seemed too loud, as if shouting rather than ringing. It was something urgent, the Jews sensed, and it was not long before they knew there was no fire that day in Novograd-Volinsk.

The bells' message that afternoon was something else; the pealing was a call to arms, a summons to take a stand against "Jewish witchcraft" and "sorcery," the signal for a pogrom.

The town's Jews, bewildered at first, ran into the street and then eventually began to congregate in makeshift hideouts, basements, and ditches. "Defense and defiance," Rabbi Korff later observed from a distance of decades in his memoir, "lay submerged under centuries of ghetto serfdom."

He recalls seeing the local Christian spiritual leader, long known as a friend to the Jews, orating from atop an upturned barrel in the town square. The boy, listening for the clergyman's impassioned attempt to calm his violent co-religionists, heard the priest's words and felt his own blood run cold. The orator was indeed impassioned, but in incitement, not containment, of the crowd. He commanded his rapt listeners to regard the economic success of the local Jewish population and then contrast it with their own miserable poverty. He charged them to exact retribution for all the disdain the Jew had no doubt harbored for them, their church, and their savior over the years.

As the crowd grew larger, the invective grew uglier. "The Jew is corrupt to the bone," the priest barked, "a reptile, fighting the forces of salvation with Satan's weapons.

"Look at him! He is different, a diabolic beast with the mark of Cain!

"His synagogues are brothels! Burn, destroy the brothels!"

Elsewhere in the city the scene was duplicated. The Jew was branded a child of the devil, and all who were willing to "avenge the cross" were assured of divine consecration.

The church bells tolled their assent and set the pace for the beatings, pillage, rape, and murder that ensued that September day. Christian bells sounded the call for human sacrifice.

In a corner of the terrified Jewish section of town, a woman with a baby in her arms and three older children in tow, scurried for safety. One of the children, a boy, stumbled and hit the pavement, bloodying his knee. The shock of seeing his mother continue to run despite his own fall obscured the pain of his skinned knee; insult, however, quickly crystallized into fear. The boy picked himself up and ran to catch up with his fleeing mother. When he heard gunfire, he turned and saw men and women, children and animals fall to the ground behind him. Blood stained the street, pooling here and there in the dirt, while cries of "Kill the Jews!" filled the air.

Then, turning back toward his family, the boy saw a bullet catch his mother; she swayed and fell on her back amid a pile of broken furniture. Nearby, a man moaned his last "Hear, O Israel." The children huddled together with their mother, who exhorted them to remain quiet and keep their heads down. When the infant she still held began to whimper, she bared her breast to nurse him. The older boy felt numb at the sight of the puddle of his mother's blood that swelled around his elbow where he lay.

"It's only a flesh wound, Boruch'l," his mother reassured him. "Just remain still, say nothing at all." And so the family lay and listened, to the cries and the moans and the church bells. Only when night fell did the relentless tolling finally cease. Mother and children remained still, the woman half-asleep, the youngsters watching wide-eyed as scavengers walked among the bodies in the moonlight, removing shoes, clothes, and valuables from the dead. The mother issued a premonition to the boy. "I bequeath you the years I was to live, my son," she sobbed, as one scavenger approached them. Ignoring the terrified children, the thief fixed his sight on their mother's diamond earrings, and, with both hands, tore them simultaneously from her ears. The woman's eyes opened suddenly and wide as the unexpected, intense pain emerged from her mouth in a piercing scream. The startled pillager dropped his booty, staggered, then stepped back and drew his pistol.

The woman's shriek died away and a cold silence reigned. The baby, momentarily disturbed from his sleep, returned, oblivious, to his mother's breast as the other children stared in horror.

"The Child is father of the Man." Baruch Korff, age five, shortly before the death of his mother in 1919.

Rabbi Korff researching his family's history at the municipal archives, Zhitomir, Ukraine, September 1994.

Gittelle Goldman Korff (1891–1919), the author's mother.

Searching for his mother's grave at the cemetery in Novograd-Volinski, September 1994.

Baruch Korff and nephew Paul S. Gass at the tomb of their distinguished ancestor, Israel Baal Shem Tov, the founder of Hasidism. Medzhibozh, Ukraine, September 1994.

"*Zhydovskaya morda,*" the man snarled. Then, only miraculously missing the suckling infant, he emptied his pistol into the woman's body.

"Die, Jew."

Though Baruch may still have looked like a terrified, helpless little boy, that was the moment he began to become a man.

Rabbi Korff's words, from his memoir:

Congealed with fear, my limbs shriveled. "Coward, coward!" cried a voice on the rebound. There was something odd about the voice. It was not human. Driven by the wind, it was strange and mystic, coming from behind the cloud that lined the far end of the sky. "Coward, coward, coward."

Other images from the life of Rabbi Korff the man emerge in sequence:

His ceaseless war-years petitioning of heads of European states, as well as the United States Congress, Supreme Court justices, and governors, demanding the rescue of Jews languishing in concentration camps.

The clandestine and dangerous negotiations he held with surrogates of Gestapo head Heinrich Himmler over the purchase of Jews from Germany for $26 a head.

The trying months in 1944 when he badgered Secretary of State Cordell Hull to move on the issue of several thousand interned European Jewish refugees. The months when Korff relentlessly enlisted President

Roosevelt's Secretary of the Treasury, Henry Morgenthau Jr. in his efforts, making the Secretary (according to Morgenthau's own diaries) physically ill for the experience. The period during which Korff pursued John Pehle, the head of the War Refugee Board, as well, waking him once at 2:00 a.m. to alert him of crucial developments and imminent death.

The outstanding success of bringing about the establishment of a reception center for Holocaust refugees at Oswego, New York, was given recognition, May 16, 1944, in the *Congressional Record*, in which Representative Thomas Lane of Massachusetts said: "Rabbi Korff has been working untiringly for the establishment of free ports of refugee for these human souls. . . The entire nation owes this man a debt of gratitude for his contribution to the various agencies of our government in helping to solve this most difficult problem."

The image of Korff utterly scandalizing his government by providing syndicated columnist Drew Pearson evidence of the State Department's unconscionable procrastination on the issue of refugees from the Holocaust.

Or the image of Korff demanding that the U.S. Air Force bomb the railroad lines leading to Auschwitz death camp, the conduit by which thousands of Jews were delivered to the ovens. On November 2, 1944, General Dwight Eisenhower informed Korff by telegram that "The conditions described in your message are well known to me. German authorities have been repeatedly and explicitly warned by radio and leaflets against committing atrocities on prisoners or civilians deportees and told that the guilty would be brought to justice."

Another image, from the summer of that same year: Korff publicly presenting a petition to House Speaker McCormack on the Capitol steps. The petition, urging that Hungarian Jews be permitted to enter Palestine, carried 500,000 signatures.

And then one from the following year, when Korff helped organize a march of 1,000 rabbis on Washington, demanding the transfer of 100,000 Jewish refugees from Europe to Palestine.

And one from the fall of 1947, when Korff was arrested in France for "terrorist activities"—an alleged plot to parachute leaflets and explosives into Great Britain in retaliation for the British refusal to allow the *Exodus–1947* to discharge its human cargo onto Palestinian shores.

And one of Korff, the following year, challenging President Truman to live up to his "pious statements" on the issue of Palestine.

Now, back to his diary *Flight From Fear*, to the young Korff, cowering in the shadow of his dying mother: "'Coward, coward, coward (came the disembodied voice).' Tears swelled my eyes and guilt settled in my heart. . . *Would these words torment me forever?*"

Knowing the life that anguished little boy subsequently came to live as an adult, his relentless commitment to principle in the face of the most daunting odds, his bold confrontation of presidents and policies, his influence on modern American history and utter refusal to so much as countenance fear in his pursuit of justice and safety for his people, one imagines not.

Regrettably, Korff's notoriety stemming from his defense of Richard Nixon has overshadowed and, at times, even eclipsed his career.

Korff, however, does not concede to have wavered in any way from his principles. To the contrary, he offers convincing evidence for the wisdom and morality of his immersion in President Nixon's cause.

I am Zamira. Baruch Korff is my father.

Index

Index

Index